Memorable Conversations

One of a kind conversations about Jesus

Glenn Murray

Endorsements

"Glenn's Memorable Conversations are not merely renditions of relational discourse but are life-giving conversations that are intended to shape our purposes and perspective about the life we have been given. After twenty years of hearing about and being involved in Glenn's "Conversations," I can truly say I know the voice of my Shepherd and how to follow Him in an intimate way. Without Glenn's example, I would just be following a set of religious rules. This is a challenging read for those who are looking to know the real Jesus."

Ryon Paton
Principal, Trinitas Partners, LLC
Private Equity Investments

"Glenn's unique life experience is the epitome of the 'ripple in a pond' – if not the ocean! His Spirit-led, well-placed conversations have positively impacted eternity for so many people. Those touched by Glenn have, in turn, enhanced the lives of untold millions. As you read Glenn's memorable conversations, may you too experience Jesus' wisdom and love ripple through your life like the tidal wave of grace that washed over Glenn."

Rick K. Pickering
Chief Executive Officer
Cal-Expo/California State Fair

"In this book, you will be listening in on some of the conversations between Glenn and his friends. Through these conversations, you will come to know the man, his love for his friends, and his love for Jesus. The more I got to know Glenn, the more I got to know Jesus. There were a couple of things that immediately drew me to Glenn. His friends happened to be many of the leaders around the world and I saw how God had used him to reach out to them. I was fascinated and a bit skeptical at the same time. It was only Glenn's words until I had a chance to join him for the Korea National Prayer Breakfast in Seoul, Korea. During my second time attending the Prayer Breakfast with Glenn, I met the former President of Korea in his office and was able to spend some time with him. As he reminisced about his relationship with Glenn, he confirmed all the stories Glenn had shared with us. President Lee, Myung bak remembered that Glenn had told him, 'Be humble, be humble, be humble.' I already trusted Glenn, but this validated his stories."

Dave Chung
Owner
Complete Copy Systems Group
Canon Dealer, Los Angeles, CA

"Glenn Murray is the most interesting person I know. From his early days as a submariner to his unabashed ministry of taking Jesus' message around the world, he has had an impact greater than most of us could imagine. He has traveled to Korea more than fifty times, receiving awards from the Korean government. His ministry has extended across the globe. Now he has written about a few of the contacts he has made throughout his life. It is compelling reading and demonstrates what one person can do when his life's mission is to follow Jesus."

Senator Tim Leslie (Ret.)
Dean of the California State Senate

"After attending a meeting at the National Hotel in Nevada City, CA, Glenn approached me as I walked to my car. That meeting, about thirty-five years ago, changed my life. Glenn's example as a brother and a friend has brought me face to face with my Lord. I have been privileged to be part of his ministry for many years. I was skeptical at first but over the years, I saw in Glenn a wisdom and a growing friendship I had not experienced with other men. I have heard many of the conversations included in this book and can attest to the fact that they are spiritually life-changing. I hope, as you read these pages, that the hearts and minds involved in the conversations will bring you peace and joy as you learn to trust Jesus."

Dr. Sam Aanestad
California State Senator (Ret.)

Conversation on a Flight to China

For many years, Vice Premier Tian Jijun has annually invited the leaders of many Asian nations to visit China for a goodwill event. Over several days, he hosts dinners and other events, including a golf tournament, with the express purpose of developing sincere friendships. Through my relationships and God-ordained circumstances, I have been one of the invitees. While traveling on China Airlines to my seventh or eighth event, I sat next to a Chinese man who was about 35 years old. Before we left the ground, I greeted him. He spoke perfect English and was very friendly. We exchanged names and he told me he had taken the American name of Mike.

After we took off and were served the customary Diet Coke and peanuts, we continued chatting. Obviously, we were both going to Shanghai. He told me that he lived in New York and had never been there. When I told him I had been there a number of times, he asked, "What is it like?" I told him, "You will feel right at home with the atmosphere because the hustle and bustle makes it feel much like New York City." That led to a very friendly and lively conversation.

Knowing a bit about Chinese culture, I noticed that he began to show me deference as he would an elderly uncle. He asked, "What is your business?" My answer to that kind of question varies because it is impossible to explain what I do in a few minutes. This time it seemed right to say, "I'm going to visit friends." He asked who I knew in Shanghai, so I mentioned the Mayor and several other high-ranking government officials from Beijing, and that piqued his interest. He asked, "Are you with the U.S. government?" I assured him that I was not and that I had no business interests in China. I was just going to visit friends. I can't remember the cause, but one of us was distracted at that point, so the conversation paused.

About fifteen minutes later, he reopened the conversation by saying, "Mr. Murray, you are much older than I am and have probably made many decisions." I quickly moved us back to a first name basis, so he said, "Glenn, I have a very important decision to make. May I ask you a question? Do you have any tips on how to make good decisions?" I asked, "What kind of decision" so he explained why he was traveling to Shanghai. He worked for Morgan Stanley, which was sending him there to open a brokerage office. However, a week before he left, Goldman Sachs called him and made him an offer to open an office for them. "I want to be loyal to my employer, but Goldman Sachs made a significantly better offer. I don't know if I should take the better offer or continue with my present plans."

keep a low profile but are free to worship God as they choose."

Mike asked a multitude of questions and seemed to have a genuine hunger to know more about God. After explaining the gospel to him in detail, I prayed with him and asked God to reveal Himself to Mike. Not being one to push a person into making a decision, I suggested that he think about these things and maybe that night in his hotel room he could invite Jesus into his heart. Again, he shocked me by saying, "I want to do that right now. Besides, wouldn't it be better to do it at 35,000 feet? I mean, we are closer to God right now." So we held hands and he had a short but earnest prayer. He said, "God, I really want to be your son. Would you let Jesus give me His life?" He may have said a few other things but those are the words that stuck with me.

After we landed and collected our luggage, I never saw him again. I did get two emails and a picture of him and his wife, who he said had also received Jesus. I never found out which company he chose but that is a minor part of this story. It was simply the means that God used for him to open his heart to Jesus. I am looking forward to meeting him again in heaven.

Conversation with an Islamic Friend

For many years, I hosted the Middle East nations at the Presidential Prayer Breakfast in Washington DC. At one of those breakfasts, I met Ahmed, who was from one of the most prominent countries in that region. He wasn't from the Royal family, but he held the highest office in their government. We spent a lot of time together that week, and I liked him immediately. As I got to know him, I learned why he was so open to talking about Jesus.

Let me give you a very condensed biographical sketch of Ahmed. Today he is fabulously wealthy (14 personal servants) but he grew up in desert poverty. Ahmed was born in one of the goatskin tents of a large Bedouin tribe. Oil was discovered in 1938, but the general population did not experience its benefits for many years. In the early nineteen forties, an evangelical missionary doctor and two nurses arrived in his area. They met with the Sheikh (Headman) of the tribe and asked if they could help with the medical needs of the people. The Sheikh was very suspicious of their motives and told his people that if they went to the clinic, they might die. However, the doctor was persistent and continued to meet with the Sheikh and explain the advances in medicine. After months of relationship building, there was a breakthrough. The Sheikh said he had a sick donkey; if the doctor could make him better, the Sheikh would allow his people to go to the clinic. We don't know how he did it, but the donkey returned to good health, so the Sheikh kept his word.

The first person he sent to the clinic was my new friend Ahmed, who was six years old at the time. He had a very serious ear infection that was draining and painful. With antibiotics and loving care, he recovered after nine days. However, one thing remained deeply ingrained in his memory. Several times a day, the nurses had whispered in his ear, "Jesus loves you." So even though he was in his sixties when I met him, our open conversations about Jesus brought back that positive memory. Because he was open to dialogue about Jesus, I invited him to a weeklong retreat later that year in the Colorado Rockies. He accepted on the spot.

He flew into Denver, and we drove up to the C-Lazy-U ranch, the only five-star dude ranch in America. Talking about Jesus (Issa/eesa) with an Islamic person is easy because the Quran mentions Him by name twenty-five times and by inference many other times. The Quran calls Him a great prophet. It affirms His virgin birth, the fact that He raised people from the dead, His second coming, and His miracles. In addition, it frequently refers to Him as Messiah. (By the way, the Quran mentions Mohammed only four times.) I knew that the Mullahs teach that one cannot be a good Muslim unless one believes in Jesus. However, by that, they mean, believe that He was a great prophet whose mother was a virgin. When you move beyond that, you quickly run into a big problem. Both the Quran and the Mullahs insist that Jesus was not the "Son of God" and was not crucified, so He did not rise from the dead. Also, when we use the term "Son of God," most followers of Islam are filled with righteous indignation because they think we mean that God had sex with Mary and that Jesus is the son. Some even want to cut your throat for insulting God.

So early in our discussions, I told Ahmed, "While we are together I will likely refer to Jesus as the 'Son of God.' I want to tell you what I <u>do not</u> mean when I use that phrase. I do not mean, 'Allah and Mary had sex and Jesus is the son.' Let me share a metaphor that might help you understand what I mean when I use that phrase."

I said, "Ahmed, I have a thought right now, can you tell me what it is? Of course you can't until I put it into words. Then I could say that the word is the son of the thought, or the thought and the words are one. I could also say that the words represent the thought or that they are the expression of the thought. The Bible uses these very same ideas to help us understand Jesus. It says, 'In the beginning was the Word and the Word was with God, and the Word was God.' (John 1:1) It says He is the full expression of God: 'The Son radiates God's own glory and expresses the very character of God…' (Heb. 1:3) Jesus himself said, 'The Father and I are one.'" (John 10:30)

Ahmed said, "I can believe He is the 'Son of God' like that."

We dialogued quite a bit about the death, burial, and resurrection. Then the Holy Spirit did what only He can do.

Questions and denials seemed to melt away. Ahmed said, "If that is really true, I am ready for God to help me believe it."

On the third morning, he told me that he believed Jesus was God's son and had paid the penalty for his sin. We chatted a bit more, then prayed together, and Ahmed became a brother in Christ.

For the remaining days, our conversation changed to include more talk of discipleship. At the end of that week, Ahmed asked if I would spend time with his family and tell his sons about Jesus.

A few months later, I traveled to _____ and spent several weeks with Ahmed and his family. I was with them every day and evening but spent my nights as his guest in a seven-star hotel. After a couple days, I asked Baqir, his thirty-six-year-old son, to show me around the area. As we were riding around, I told him how much I loved his dad and that I was glad we'd had a chance to get to know each other. I told him that in preparation for my visit I had read the Quran and had developed some questions.

He quickly said, "Have you really read the Quran?"

I said, "Yes, I've read the English version twice."

He asked, "Do you want to become a Muslim?"

My answer shocked him, as it will most people who read this. I told him, "I'm already a 'muslim.'" When he looked at me with a puzzled look, I said, "The word 'muslim' is Arabic. What does it mean in English?"

He said it meant, "One who submits to God." *(Note: "m*uslim*" with a lowercase "m" means one who submits to God, while "Muslim" with a capital "M" means a follower of Islam.)*

I said, "That's my understanding as well. If you were speaking Arabic and introduced me to a friend, I hope you would say, 'Glenn is a *muslim* (submitted to God), but he's a disciple of Jesus, not Mohammed.'"

Then I said, "If you could help me be a better 'muslim' (more surrendered to God), I'd like that."

He quickly said, "If you want to be a good Muslim, you must understand that Abraham did not sacrifice Isaac. He sacrificed Ishmael."

Now we could have had a debate, with me saying, "It was Isaac," and him saying, "It was Ishmael." We would likely not have resolved that issue quickly, so I sidestepped it. I said, "Don't you remember? Neither boy was sacrificed. God provided a sacrifice out of the bushes, and it was a ram."

He said, "Oh yeah." I continued; "In fact, you still sacrifice animals annually during Ramadan at the Kaaba (Black Cube) in Mecca. Why don't you ask your Mullah (Head of your

Mosque), 'What is the purpose of a blood sacrifice?'" Over the next two weeks, we had several conversations about this.

I also knew that if I told someone that I had read the Quran, they would want to know whether I was able to read and write Arabic. If I said I didn't, they would make it clear that I had not read the true version because the Arabic language and the Quran are one. So I said, "I read an English translation of the Quran, and I want to check with you to see if things I found in my English translation are in the original."

He said, "Okay, of course."

I said, "The Quran mentions the 'Injeel' (The Gospels) many, many times and it is clear that Mohammed read them. Is that true in the Arabic version?"

He said, "Yes, that's correct."

I asked, "Have you read the 'Injeel'?"

He said, "No, I have never seen them."

When I asked why, his answer was: "The Jews corrupted the Old Testament, and the Christians corrupted the New Testament, so they're not trustworthy. If I had the 'Injeel' that Mohammed read, I would definitely read it."

When he said the "Injeel" was corrupted, I said, "I guess that's theoretically possible. I personally do not believe it was changed because I believe the Holy Spirit of God protected it. However, to be intellectually honest, I must admit the possibility that the New Testament could have been changed. That's because I am aware that we do not have any originals of the New Testament. All we have are copies of copies of copies. The oldest complete copy we have is 300 years after Jesus. Nevertheless, I can take you to the British Museum in London or the Vatican in Rome and prove that it has not changed since about 300 AD. Therefore, if it was changed, it was changed in those first 300 years." I told him, "You can't believe how excited I got when I learned from the Quran that the 'Injeel' was still trustworthy according to Mohammed in 625 AD. He gives me a 300-year overlap to help me trust my Bible."

He seemed unconvinced about that, so I gave him a challenge. "Why don't you call your pilot and tell him to prepare the Gulfstream V jet. Let's go to the British Museum."

He said, "We won't have to do that. I believe you." I gave him a copy of the Arabic New Testament, and he committed to reading the Injeel.

I can't give you the eventual result of this conversation with Ahmed's son because I don't know the end of that story. My only reason for writing this is to report a memorable conversation I had with an Islamic man and his son.

Actually, I think I will relate a bit more about Ahmed. A couple years before I visited Ahmed, I spoke at a ten-day retreat at a beautiful old castle near Brighton, England. It was called the Third Arab World Congress and included 200 attendees from seven Middle Eastern nations. A group of friends and extended families who were both followers of Jesus and followers of Mohammed had put it together. There I met a number of amazing men who had secret house churches in their home countries. One man was named Yusef, and he was from Ahmed's country. A few days after I arrived, I contacted him and introduced them to each other. Twice, Ahmed and I went to Yusef's secret house church after very covert arrangements. They became friends and could meet publicly because Yusef was a prominent business executive. The three weeks I spent with Ahmed and his family remain one of my treasured memories.

I stayed in touch with Ahmed, and a year and a half after I returned home, I got a phone call from Washington DC. It was Ahmed. He was ecstatic and yelled, "Glenn, I feel compete, I feel complete. Dick Halverson baptized me in the pool at the Cedars." What a joy to hear that my mentor had baptized Ahmed.

Conversation with an Israeli Politician

During the years that I hosted the Middle Eastern nations at the Presidential Prayer Breakfast in Washington DC, I met and became friends with attendees from a dozen countries in that region. Many invited me to visit them and I accepted most of the invitations. On my first trip, I spent three weeks in Kuwait and a week each in Jordan, Palestine, Egypt, Morocco, and Israel. God gave me favor with numerous leaders of those nations and I had the opportunity to have substantive conversations about Jesus with them.

I have a multitude of wonderful events and conversations to report from that and subsequent visits, but for this article, I want to concentrate on two men. One was a senior Palestinian leader. The other was an official of the Israeli government. While they knew much about each other, they had never met face to face. To my knowledge, that is still true today. Both had a lifetime of experience with the Israeli/Palestinian conflict and had lived through and participated in several of the Middle Eastern wars. As I write about my interactions with them, I have changed their names to guard their identities. I am confident they would be uncomfortable if the content of our conversations became public.

One evening, while I had dinner with "Fadi Habib," an official of the PLO (Palestine Liberation Organization), he told me five or six stories about Jewish atrocities. One of those happened in 1967 when Israel's Arab neighbors attacked it during the Six-Day War, also known as the Third Arab-Israeli War. On the first day of that war, Fadi was near the Damascus Gate and saw an Israeli tank coming down the street. The driver saw a Palestinian boy, around six years old, walking alone; the driver swerved onto the sidewalk and ran over the boy. Then the driver went forward and back several times. When the tank moved on, nothing was left on the sidewalk but a blood spot. Fadi and his wife wept as he recalled that experience. His hatred of the Jews was palpable. There were several other stories but that will suffice to illustrate how much animosity exists between the Israelis and the Palestinians. By the way, Fadi accepted my invitation to attend the President's Prayer Breakfast in Washington the following year. I met with him after that breakfast and he was very moved and exceedingly open to speaking about Jesus.

The morning after that dinner with Fadi and his wife "Melita," I had breakfast with "Aron Goldberg" and his wife, "Leah," in the breakfast nook of their lovely home in Jerusalem. Aron is a highly visible and respected official in the Israeli Cabinet. After a few minutes of small talk, our conversation turned to a recent newspaper article about a Palestinian threat. This led him to share an equal number of stories about Palestinian atrocities. He told me that he had been the first person to arrive on the scene after an attack on an elementary school by a terrorist group. The terrorists had thrown explosives through several windows and doors, killing seventy children. He said body parts were everywhere and not one child's body was intact. As he provided more details about the scene, Leah started to weep but Aron remained stoic. This was not the first time he had seen the results of a terrorist attack. He said for reasons of self-preservation, he had learned to control his emotions without denying his feelings.

This led to a lengthy discussion about the multitude of terrorist attacks that Israel had endured since 1948. At the appropriate time, I told Aron about my dinner the night before and that I had heard the same kind of stories from the other side. I said, "I believe both of you are telling me the truth. These memories of atrocities are passed from generation to generation, with extreme distrust and hatred being the result."

I asked him if he could conceive of anything that would create a breakthrough in the relationship between Palestinian and Jew. I suggested that he not let thoughts or comments like "We tried that" or "That would never work" keep him from letting his mind process the possibilities. He paused for several seconds, as if he were thinking deeply, then said, "I can't think of anything. Too many people have died." I told him, "In my opinion, the only possible answer is the reconciling love of Jesus." He responded very quickly, saying, "I don't have anything against Jesus, just some

Christians." I replied just as quickly, "I can understand that, Aron, but Jesus wasn't a Christian."

His immediate response was, "What did you say?" The statement seemed to bewilder him. Then he looked at the ceiling and repeated it over and over: "Jesus wasn't a Christian. Wow, Jesus wasn't a Christian. Then to his wife: "Leah, Jesus wasn't a Christian." I think he must have said that seven or eight times. It was a moment I shall never forget. I found myself saying, "Aron, I am stunned at why that affected you as it did. However, I will acknowledge that most 'Christians' would also be shocked if I said it to them." Nevertheless, it's a historical fact that "Jesus wasn't a Christian," and while it sounds bizarre, on reflection it is indisputable. Jesus was a Jew and his followers were not called "Christians" until forty years after He left the earth. Therefore, He couldn't have been a "Christian." It is a well-documented fact that His followers were first called Christians while Paul and Barnabas were in Antioch. (Acts 11:26 - 43AD) I am certain that Aron knew intellectually that Jesus was a Jew. However, in tennis terms, Christians had Jesus on their "side of the net," and since Aron would never consider becoming a Christian, he couldn't consider the claims of Jesus. For that moment in time, I took down the net, which allowed him to process the life of Jesus in a new way.

I asked, "Do you think Jesus was a real person or a fictitious character? Obviously, you don't think He is divine or the Messiah, but do you believe He was a historical figure?" His answer was quick and very matter of fact: "Of

25

course I believe he lived. He was born six miles from my house," as he pointed with his thumb towards Bethlehem. I said, "What is your candid opinion about that man who was born six miles from your house?" He said, "I think He was a good Rabbi (teacher) and a man of peace." Formerly, my response would have been that He couldn't have been a good teacher if he had lied to us ... you know, the "Liar, Lunatic, or Lord" proposition that C.S. Lewis popularized in his book, *Mere Christianity*. I suppose that is useful in some situations, but I found myself saying, "You know, I also think He was a great teacher." We really do, don't we? But we believe He is more than a teacher. In fact, he is the Son of God. Nevertheless, can't we give a person permission to think of Him as a good teacher as a place to start? That's what I did.

"Aron, you said that you believe He was a good teacher; could I press you to define that a bit more? How would you compare Jesus to the great moral, ethical, and spiritual teachers of history? I know you will consider Moses but don't forget Socrates, Plato, and Aristotle." He thought for a moment, then said, "Jesus was probably the greatest teacher who ever lived." Because we were in total agreement on this, I told him that the teaching of Jesus had changed my life and I added a few thoughts about being His disciple. Then I said, "Since by your own self-definition you believe He was the greatest teacher who ever lived, how much do you know about what He taught? He said, "Practically nothing." Then he laughed out loud and said, "That doesn't make any sense, does it?" I said, "No, it doesn't. I bet you could tell me something that Plato taught." He said, "You're right, I probably should know more about what Jesus taught." Then he asked, "What do you think I should do?"

I proposed that he start with Flavius Josephus, the Jewish historian who wrote a book called *The Antiquities of the Jews*. Josephus lived just a few years after Jesus and was a Jewish scholar and one of Israel's greatest historians. He studied with the Sadducees, Pharisees, and Essenes but eventually aligned himself with the Pharisees. I told Aron that his book reported a bit about Jesus, but that there was a better option. Jesus had a best friend who wrote a book about Him. I suggested that he get that book and read it. Aron seemed sincere when he asked, "What is the name of that book?" I answered, "The book of John in the New Testament." He said, "Oh yes, I've heard about that, but I have never read it." I encouraged him to read the book that Jesus' best friend wrote and to evaluate the teachings of Jesus for himself.

I went on to say, "You will have a hard time believing many of the things that John reports about Jesus but at least you will know what his best friend says He taught." Aron said he would start reading John's book so he could know at least something about what the greatest teacher in history taught. I cannot report how the Holy Spirit used the words of Scripture in Aron's life because I never saw him again. I'm confident, however, that because he committed to reading the book of John, God's Holy Spirit will speak to him. I pray that Aron allowed the Holy Spirit to open his heart to Jesus, though, of course, his response is between himself and God.

This, like many of the conversations I have had throughout the years, did not result in some closure of which I am aware. However, my intent in writing about it was simply to recount a memorable conversation and how the Lord allowed me to be a witness for Jesus.

Conversations at a Private "Off-the-Record" Dinner

Because I was a close friend of the host, he invited me to join a group of ten men for dinner at his home in San Francisco. He told me who would be attending, and I felt privileged to be included. The guest of honor was a "name-in-the-news" U.S. State Department official. His visit was for only one evening and was not part of his public calendar. The others were presidents and CEOs of international corporations. Two had flown in from the East Coast that day, while the rest were from California. Several of the men already knew each other quite well, so I think my friend thought he had to justify why he had invited me. He introduced me as a trusted friend who had met with heads of state and leaders in politics and business around the world. I seemed to be accepted, and he made me feel very comfortable to be there. He went on to explain that each invitee was chosen because of his deep knowledge of a specific region of the world. That made me feel less comfortable, but I knew God had a purpose for my being there.

At dinner, our host explained that the State Department person had initiated the evening to get feedback about trade and the geopolitical implications of our foreign policy. He told us that the guest of honor wanted to hear each man's candid, off-the-record opinions. That created an atmosphere of openness which provoked some intense discussions. Special emphasis was placed on the hot spots around the globe. The man from the State Department told us that forty-six active shooting wars were going on at that very moment. The conversation was free-flowing about diverse topics, and genuine wisdom was expressed, which made each discussion seem very constructive. After three-and-a-half hours of spirited dialogue, there was a momentary pause in the conversation. At that point, our host turned to me and said, "Glenn, you have been unusually quiet tonight. I know you well enough to know that you must have some thoughts on these issues."

I did indeed, so I shared the following. "I am very impressed by the magnitude of knowledge you men have about the world, and how much you care about finding solutions. I know these conflicts affect your day-to-day decisions, so it motivates me to pray for you. As I've listened to you speak about the current state of affairs, I think you have described them accurately, and in my opinion, your insights are flawless. However, though you have defined them correctly, I didn't hear any lasting solutions.

"I think we can all agree that most serious conflicts are not just people with a difference of opinion. Their issues are not intellectual; they are visceral, gut level, they hate each other. When you use words like love and hate, you are speaking about matters of the heart, not the head. If our efforts do not address the human heart, we have short-term, unreliable solutions. The United Nations and U.S. Diplomatic Corps are highly skilled and designed to appeal to rational people and negotiate an equitable solution to difficult situations. However, if the root cause is hate, negotiation will rarely solve the conflicts. Therefore, we often have to send in troops, but they are not expected to solve the problem; they are meant only to keep it from getting worse."

I reminded them of a recent study authorized by the Joint Chiefs of Staff at the Pentagon. The study categorically stated that the world's number-one problem was alienation. I said, "That is true at every level of society, and reconciliation is desperately needed. So let me be so bold as to suggest what I believe is the answer. I've discussed it with senior business and political leaders around the world, so let me start by giving you the opinion of two of those leaders. These men are at the very center of a couple of the world's most intractable problems."

I recalled for them a meeting I'd had with Supreme Court Justice Esteban Bendek from Colombia. As we discussed the drug problem, I asked, "Will there ever be a solution?" He said, "Glenn, we have tried many things, but nothing works for very long." We were having dinner, and he put his clenched fist on the table with his thumb raised. Then he pushed his thumb down with his other hand. He put his other clenched fist on the table with the thumb sticking up and proceeded to push down that thumb. He repeated this several times and said, "Every time we push it down in one place, it pops up in another." Then Esteban volunteered that the only answer he could think of would require that people have a change of heart.

The second person I spoke about was Netanel Lorch, the Secretary General of the Israeli Knesset. He had invited me to a private dinner at his home in Jerusalem, and we had a lengthy and very thorough discussion about the Israeli-Arab conflict. By any measure, he was an expert on the issues and attitudes of the Middle East. He had worked on the Israeli-Arab conflict for years, and one of his greatest achievements was convincing President Sadat of Egypt to speak at the Knesset. At one point, he expressed his frustration at an inability to find lasting solutions. He volunteered that the hostilities would continue until people had a change of heart.

Both of these leaders were secular, non-religious men using terminology normally reserved for pastors. However, after working closely with the most serious problems of our day, they had concluded that the true problem was the condition of the human heart.

I suggested that the number-one authority on reconciliation was Jesus. He said that giving and receiving of forgiveness was the answer, but that requires a change of heart. Then I suggested that He could change any individual's heart. "I know that from personal experience because He gave me a new heart."

At that point, in a sarcastic tone, one of the most prominent CEO's said, "Oh my God, does that mean everyone has to become a Christian before we can find a way to live in peace?" I answered, "I was not talking about religion because it is often part of the problem. Because religion has caused so many needless divisions in our world, I was not promoting it as an answer. I was talking about Jesus of Nazareth, not a religion. Secondly, I don't believe every person must follow Jesus for us to make some progress on reconciliation. People follow leaders, so let me ask a question.

"How many leaders do you think there are in the entire world? I mean leaders who make the macro decisions to which others must respond." The first man said, "There are around twenty." That started a discussion, and the group ultimately settled on just eight alpha leaders in the world.

I noted that a very small number of people provided leadership in every subdivision of culture, whether we were talking about an inner-city gang or the United Nations. "I know personally that there are only two or three unchallenged leaders within the thousands of gang members in Los Angeles. People follow leaders, and there are likely only a small number of leaders in every unit of society. This is true for the Rotary Club, a country club, your church, a Boy Scout troop, or an international corporation.

"The need of the hour is for some of these leaders to have a change of heart. If that happened and they became authentic followers of Jesus, they would find themselves becoming more servant leadership oriented. History has shown that only when we have this kind of selfless leadership can we expect to see real solutions. It will never be a perfect world, but it could be much different and more hopeful than it is now. The question is, do you agree that the most troublesome problems of our world really are matters of the heart?"

Just then, the man from the State Department said, "Glenn, does anyone else in the whole world think like you do?" My response was, "Oh yes. You must be hanging out with the wrong people." Then he said, in a *gotcha* tone, "Anyone in DC?" I said, "Yes, I could introduce you to a number of friends in DC who think like I do." Two weeks later, I introduced him to a few friends. He became a regular in a group that meets every Tuesday to study the life of Jesus.

As the meeting broke up, one of the men from the East Coast said, "You had some friends in DC who think like you. Do you have any in New York City?" I said yes. This man asked to walk me to my car and I wound up taking him back to the Fairmont Hotel. As we sat in the car in front of the hotel, he asked, "Would you come to New York City and tell my friends what we talked about tonight?" I agreed, so two months later, he flew Mary Ann and me to New York City and put us up in the Marriott Marquis hotel. We spent a week in one-on-one meetings and small group gatherings. This man started each meeting with an explanation of our San Francisco dinner. He then introduced me and said, "Tell them what you told us that evening."

I could write several pages of memories about the prominent business and legal people we met. One was the owner of the world's largest container ship company. Another was a man from Saudi Arabia who handled all the real estate for the Royal Family. We spent an entire day with him and had substantive conversations about Jesus. He told us about his hometown and the health of his mother, then began to cry when we held hands and prayed for her and his family. Through the tears he said, "No one has ever prayed for my mother." While there, I also answered my host's original question: "Do you have anyone in New York City?" I introduced him to an associate of mine, and they have been meeting one on one for some time now.

There is no way to know exactly how God will use that evening or the spin-offs that came from it. However, it was fun to simply go with the flow as He opened doors and gave me the opportunity to represent Jesus in that setting.

Conversations with My Friend
Gi Kwang Sunim

Chief Buddhist Monk of Korea

For my family and friends, I feel the need to preserve the history of my relationship with a man who represents a completely different view of spirituality than I have. In spite of this, I grew to love and respect him. Sadly, he passed away a year ago, and I still miss him. As I reflect on our time together, I realize that I learned a good deal about Buddhism. However, because his questions were so different from anything I had ever encountered, I also learned much more about my own faith. Early in our relationship, we gave each other permission to ask any question about our respective faiths but without the intent to convert one another. His questions were always challenging, and he said mine were as well. They caused me to rely on the Holy Spirit at a new level. Almost every time I answered his questions, the answer was something I had never thought about. Giving a complete report of our hours of dialogue would be impossible, so this will be a series of mostly unconnected anecdotes with personal confidential information omitted.

After several years of developing relationships in South Korea, I had met a few pastors and church leaders, but most of my friends were businessmen or politicians. They represented the spectrum of religious persuasions and included people from every major Christian denomination, as well as a number of secularists plus numerous practicing and non-practicing Buddhists. Because so many were Buddhist, and I knew so little about Buddhism, I had some catching up to do. I read some books but mostly let the men with whom I met educate me about what they believed. I had some very profound discussions with CEOs and legislators who were practicing Buddhists. They told me about the Eightfold Path, which is the Middle Path, consisting of Right Speech, Right Action, Right Livelihood, Right Effort, Right Mindfulness, Right Concentration, Right Understanding, and Right Thoughts. The Middle Path is a righteous way of life for self-purification, and it depends on strict self-discipline.

Many of the men I knew were very connected. By that, I mean they seemed to know everyone. One day I told one of them that I wanted to meet a person whom at that time I called "The Buddhist Pope." The man explained to me that the person about whom I was speaking was Gi Kwang Sunim, the Chief Buddhist Monk of Korea. Of course, the man knew him, and even though this man was a Christian, he arranged an introduction. The rest of this chapter will relate a series of exchanges between us during our twelve-year friendship. Except for the first or second meetings, I'm not certain about the chronological sequence of the conversations, but their content is quite fresh in my mind.

Our very first encounter was in the Chief Monk's office, which was a five-story glass and stone building with two or three levels of parking underneath it. It was an office building with a temple on the middle floors and his office was modestly furnished. The Chief Monk's desk was similar to a coffee table, and he sat on the floor. He had chairs for guests, but mostly I sat on the floor with him. I could easily understand him because he spoke English quite well. I thanked him for accepting a stranger's request to meet with him.

He said, "I respect your friend very much, so when he asked me for an appointment I immediately said yes because I knew his friend would be someone who would be worth meeting." Early in that conservation, he asked, "Did you have a reason for wanting to meet me?"

"Yes," I replied. "I've been to Korea a number of times, and many of my friends are Buddhists. I felt it important to meet the person who leads the Buddhists in Korea. I am not here to become a Buddhist, nor am I here to convert you. Of course, I am open to any questions about my faith but that is not why I came. I simply have a desire to learn more about what you believe."

My friend had introduced me as a person who was very serious about following Jesus and said that I represented the Congressional Committee that hosted the United States

Presidential Prayer Breakfast. Assuming that I knew the President, the monk asked me to thank him for sending a letter of congratulations regarding the anniversary of World Buddhism. I told him that I was not a personal friend of the President but suggested that if he wrote a thank-you letter and attended our National Prayer Breakfast, I could arrange for him to hand deliver it. Unfortunately, his schedule did not allow him to ever accept that offer.

As I look back, I think this early exchange set the stage for our friendship because he asked questions about my involvement with the Presidential Prayer Breakfast and wanted to know its purpose. I gave him a bit of its history and explained that leaders from approximately 170 nations attended. I said that it had no political, business, or religious agenda but simply met in the spirit of Jesus. I spent another five minutes telling him what that meant. It was not a monologue because he asked some very pointed questions that gave me a chance to share my life in Jesus. After about twenty minutes, he asked if he could bring in some other monks to listen to our conversation.

I said, "Yes, please do." He brought in three senior monks and spoke to them in Korean.

My friend interpreted it for me: "He is telling them that you are the first person who ever spoke to him about Jesus who didn't make him feel like an enemy." When the Chief Monk finished speaking with the other monks, I told him that my friend had interpreted for me what he had said to them.

Then I added, "I'm sure glad you caught me on a good day." I explained that when a person is excited about something, he might speak of it so exuberantly that it could make another person feel as though what he had was a pile of dirt. I used the example of a person who owned a Lexus automobile extolling its virtues so strongly that anyone with a Mercedes felt like what he had was inferior. I went on to say, "I am so devoted to Jesus that I must have made someone, somewhere feel like the enemy, but I am glad you didn't feel that from me."

For another thirty minutes, we continued talking about many things. Much of our discussion was about him personally. Eventually, there was a lull in our conversation and I said, "I would like to return to your earlier statement that I didn't make you feel like the enemy. As I have listened to you, I've been thinking, *How do I feel about this new friend?* I certainly do not think of you as an enemy, and from the comments you've made, I've concluded that you're my brother."

The friend who had brought me was a Christian, and I'm sure he was shocked to hear me say that. I explained myself: "Do you know that there are many brotherhoods in the world? There is a brotherhood around Rotary, golf, fishing, fraternities in college, and many sports. There is also a brotherhood around Jesus, and our mutual friend and I are brothers in that family. However, the brotherhood I feel with you is different from all those. As I have listened to you, it seems like you're a man who would not want to get to the end of your life and have it based on error. That's the way I feel as well. So I think that you and I are brothers in that brotherhood of men who want to base their life on truth."

He got up, walked two or three steps to shake my hand, and said, "Okay, we're brothers in that brotherhood."

I said, "Gi Kwang, I think Buddha was one of our brothers. He was the son of the king in Nepal; however, though he was a prince, he left his comfortable existence and went on a six-and-a-half-year search for truth and the meaning of life. It's very unfortunate that he lived 600 years before Jesus, who said, 'I am the truth.' When I read the *Golden Book* by Mahendra Kulasrestha, it was obvious that Buddha was searching for truth. I believe that if he had been alive during the days of Jesus, he would have gone to listen to him. I don't know if he would have become a disciple, but knowing what motivated him, I believe if someone had stood up near him and said, 'I am the truth,' he would have gone to listen and evaluate. Of course, I believe that Buddha would want you to do the same thing."

During our second meeting, I told him what I had been thinking about on my flight to Seoul. "I was trying to understand what is happening between Gi Kwang Sunim and Glenn Murray when we are so different. You're Oriental; I'm Occidental. You're from the East; I'm from the West. Your culture is several thousand years old, and mine is 200 years old. Therefore, I came up with a metaphor that helped me understand what is happening between us. It's as if we are from two countries separated by a river, and you and I have built a bridge over it. We can meet in the middle of the bridge and ask each other questions about the worlds we represent."

He understood my metaphor immediately and said, "I'll meet you in the middle of the bridge, and I get the first question." His first question rather shocked me because I thought it would be something theological. His question was: "Why are there so many divorces in your country?" I agreed with him that there were too many divorces in my country, and the result had left many children and families devastated.

I said that Jesus disapproved of divorce and formerly his followers were not the ones who got divorced. However, in this last generation, divorces were almost as common in the church as they are among people who are unbelievers. We spoke a little more about this subject. Then I said, "I get the next question. You told me that you pray several times a day; my question is, 'To whom do you pray?'" He replied, "Buddha."

"That leaves me a bit confused." I said, "I've read that you believe Buddha reached Nirvana, the life of a snuffed-out candle, the extinguished life or the life of nothingness. Are you saying that you pray to someone who doesn't exist?"

He tilted his head to the side and said, "It's kind of hard to understand, isn't it?"

I said, "Yes" but didn't press the point. In a later conversation about prayer, we pursued this subject in depth.

During another of our conversations, I told him, "I admire Buddha for many things, particularly his desire for truth and his call for a life of purity, no adultery, no stealing, no lying, etc. I really liked the chapter in the *Golden Book* on fellowship and dying to self. Buddha taught that one must die to self, but he didn't know anything beyond that. For him, Nirvana was death to self-desire. Jesus also taught that we must die to self, but when we receive Him, He gives us His life, which is eternal. Buddha and Confucius both saw the kind of morality that is correct but left to human resources; we're not capable of living like that. Jesus comes into our lives and gives us the power to do what is right."

He said, "Glenn, you know a lot about Buddhism, but I don't think you know the deep things of Buddhism."

I said, "I'm sure I don't. Is there something I should know?"

"Yes. In a book the monks read, called *Who I Am*, there is a statement that says, 'If on your road to truth you encounter Buddha, kill Buddha.'" He explained that it was a metaphor; one should not let anything keep one from the truth. Go around him, push him out of the way, etc., but the metaphor is, kill Buddha. Then, during one of my first encounters with his penetrating questions, he asked, "If you and I are going to be brothers in that brotherhood of men who base their lives on truth, would you kill Jesus?"

I answered, "Wow! I've never faced a question like that, but given the context of your question, my answer must be 'yes.' If Jesus keeps me from knowing the truth, then my answer is a definite 'Yes.' However, my Bible and my own personal experience tell me that truth is not beyond Jesus; Jesus Himself is Truth." At that time, I didn't know the monk well, so to make my point I asked a question that now seems silly: "Do you know what a birthday candle is?"

He quickly said, "Yes" and indicated how small they are.

I said, "If you light a birthday candle in a universe of darkness, the darkness cannot put it out because light always overcomes darkness. It may be a small area, but light always prevails. Gi Kwang, Jesus said, "I am the Light of the World." If a universe of darkness cannot put out a candle, nothing can extinguish the Light of the World. Therefore, the real answer to your question is that I couldn't kill Jesus if I wanted to because I don't know how to extinguish the Light of the World." He understood the metaphor and didn't pursue it further.

One day he said, "Glenn, we're becoming such good friends, I should probably go to church with you someday."

I told him, "I don't have a specific church that I go to, but we can pick one and attend together." As I thought about it later, I realized that attending church together would be a mistake because a Buddhist monk walking into any church would cause a great disturbance.

He said, "If I go to church with you, will you go to the Temple with me?"

He was quite surprised that I answered "yes" because the Korean pastor of the largest church in the world had said that no believer should go inside a temple because it's full of idols.

I told him, "I'm not sure that I should go in temples, but I've been in so many in Thailand, Taiwan, Japan and other places that I would be willing to go with you to your temple."

He asked, "If I go to your church, I will bow before I go in. Would you bow before you go in the Temple?"

I got the sense that his questions were leading to a point he wanted to make. I thought for a moment, then said, "Yes, I probably would, but let me explain what I mean by that. I am not Roman Catholic but I have many friends who are. When I go to church with them, I kneel when they kneel and get up when they do. It's not my way but I do it to honor them. So if you bow before you go in the Temple, I would bow to honor you."

I was certain we were going somewhere when next he asked, "If I go to church with you, I will bow to Jesus before going in. Would you bow to Buddha before you go in the Temple?"

I said, "Gi Kwang, where do you get these questions? This is like when you asked if I would I kill Jesus." My first response was to ask him if I could I answer that on my next trip. Then I said, "No, you want an answer now, don't you? I know that if you gave me six months to think about it, I would start on the airplane going home. I would be thinking, 'I wonder what he means by *bow*,' so can I explore that with you right now? If I met a man on the road in the countryside and he was very old and had a long, wispy beard, and someone told me he had twenty grandchildren, I would bow to him out of respect for his age because that is the custom. He could be the head of the local Mafia. I wouldn't know that, but I would bow to him in deference to his age."

I added that if the leader of China went to the United States, he would shake hands with our President. It would not mean that he was in favor of capitalism, but he would shake hands because that was the way to honor the person and the office. "So if you mean to bow to Buddha by way of showing respect, I would do that quickly. I do respect Buddha and appreciate some of the things he said. But if, on the other hand, you mean bow out of allegiance, submission, adoration, or worship, I could never bow my knee to anyone like that except Jesus Christ."

He said, "Glenn, that is a very wise answer."

"If that seemed wise to you, my understanding is that it was given to me by the Holy Spirit to help you understand that I don't disrespect Buddha, but my Lord is Jesus Christ, and I bow my knee only to him."

Then he stunned me by saying, "Glenn, the next time you are in Korea would you speak to the nation about Jesus on my national radio network?" I declined and told him, "The reason is, I keep my activities in Korea below the radar because I meet so many powerful people of different political and religious persuasions. I do not want to develop a public presence in Korea, so I must decline, but thank you for asking."

Then he said, "Well, would you meet with the 'Council of Forty' the next time you're in Korea and talk to them about Jesus like we talk?" These are the top forty monks in Korea. I accepted his offer and told him I was excited to do that on my next visit.

Six months later, when I was back in Seoul, this is how the scenario developed. He picked me up in his chauffeur-driven limousine and we returned to his office in the Temple. We had tea and conversation for about an hour, then he said, "It's time to go." We went to the underground garage and his limousine, then began driving across town. I had no idea where we were going. Before long, I saw three klieg lights dancing across the sky in the direction we were traveling. As we got closer, I realized we were going to the location of those lights. It turned out to be a large convention center.

As we pulled under the portico, I noticed three or four television cameras focused on our car. When we got out, the cameras focused on me and followed me into the building. As it turned out, 6,000 people were already seated, waiting for our arrival.

We went up a few stairs into what I would consider a "loge" area where the 'Council of Forty' monks was sitting. Four visiting Tibetan monks also joined us that night. The minute we sat down, the lights went off. On the stage in front of the curtain, a spotlight appeared on a microphone. A man came out and began to speak in Korean; of course, I couldn't understand him, but eventually he said, "Glenn Murray."

Gi Kwang nudged me and told me to stand up. The crowd turned around, looked up at me, and began to cheer. The first thought that came to me was, 'God, you have a powerful sense of humor; you gather 6,000 Buddhists to honor one of your sons." Then the show started. It was a magnificent two-hour production with opera singers and folk dancers. During the intermission, I was introduced to the leader of the 'Council of Forty'. Gi Kwang told him that I was a very close friend of his. They were extremely gracious, but I had the chance to talk to only one of them in any depth. Gi Kwang never explained why he had arranged the evening but, given the things that were said, I have an opinion. He and I had become very close friends. The monks, on the other hand, were likely suspicious of me. Therefore, I concluded that he was trying to honor me in their presence to give me some level of credibility with them. I think it was his way of telling the monks that he respected me, and that they should as well. It was likely an attempt to pave the way for me to speak to them at a later date. Unfortunately, Gi Kwang passed away before we did that. Of course, I can never know for sure, but this is what I believed was happening.

One time, I asked Gi Kwang to explain reincarnation to me; it turned out to be a three-hour session. He started by saying that everything is one, all life comes from space, and everything comes from pure mind. It is the source of all energy; heaven is the highest star, and hell is a black hole. Then he started explaining reincarnation by telling me that he'd had five lives, including the one he now had, and he knew the details of the last three. He said he could also tell about other people's past lives. He began telling me about his three past lives and ended with the last one, in which he was Chinese. Suddenly, he stopped short and said, "Oh my goodness! (or something like that), Glenn, you were also Chinese in your last life. That's why I understand your metaphors so quickly; it's why you love Asians and why you think like an Oriental. That's why you and I have become such intimate friends."

I didn't laugh or give any indication that I was disagreeing. I just said, "That's a fascinating idea; tell me more about my Chinese life. Did you and I know each other, and if so, were we friends or business partners?"

He didn't have an answer but said, "I know you were Chinese in your last life."

To show you the level of our honest exchange of ideas, at that point I said to him, "You know I don't believe in reincarnation but I have an alternative opinion about why you feel close to me. My thought is that you live in a world where anybody who loves Jesus considers you an enemy. You know I genuinely love you and because my love comes from Jesus, my view of why you feel close to me is that you feel the love of Jesus."

His response was, "It's possible." This was an implicit admittance that maybe it was not our former Chinese lives that made us close but rather the fact that he felt loved.

I added, "Not only do I love you but Jesus loves you as well." In all our conversations that had this kind of content,

I never pressed for winning the point; I simply made the statement and we moved on.

Gi Kwang told me, "The most influential pastor in Korea said that Buddhists are an evil influence on the culture. He has taught people to hate the Buddhist and most pastors have done the same." I can't vouch for the validity of this statement, but it is true that many church people in Korea think and speak negatively about Buddhists.

To illustrate this, I'll share an experience I had while speaking to legislators at their capitol, which is called the National Assembly Building. The influential pastor Gi Kwang mentioned had fifteen minutes, and I had fifteen minutes. The pastor spoke first and used almost the same words that Gi Kwang had told me.

He spoke about how the Buddhists had a negative influence on the culture and were the enemy of the church. I changed what I had planned to talk about and said, "It's possible that the Buddhists are the church's enemy, but they are not the enemy of Jesus." I went on to say that I considered Gi Kwang Sunim to be a good friend; of course, they all knew who he was. I said Jesus loved him as much as He loved the pastor and me. I was later told that my comments hadn't alienated the pastor. At least it did not seem to fracture our relationship.

One day, as we talked about how unique our relationship was, Gi Kwang said that he'd never had a friend to whom he felt closer. I told him that we could say that we were intimate friends, and he loved the word *intimate*. From then on he said many times, "I feel so intimate with you." That was proven over time because, in fact, he shared deeply private things about himself and his personal history. He had been Chief Monk for some time when I met him at approximately sixty-five years of age. He told me his life story, and I will share a bit of that which is public knowledge.

After he graduated from college, he was a twenty-two-year-old Buddhist newspaper reporter with some internal struggles. He was counseled to spend a month or two at a Buddhist monastery and retreat at the top of one of Korea's mountains. He ended up staying six years, became a monk, and left the monastery to move to Seoul. His leadership, entrepreneurial skills, and vision attracted attention. Over time, he rose in the ranks to lead the thousands of temples and multiple thousands of monks. My evaluation was that he had exceptional organizational, fundraising, and leadership abilities.

One time we were meeting in his office and discussing a broad range of subjects. I think he read The Wall Street Journal every morning because he was very aware of what was happening around the world. After a few minutes, the Holy Spirit prompted me to raise the issue of prayer again. I said, "Gi Kwang, we have become such good friends that I feel like I can ask you a very challenging question. I will tell you in advance, however, that I love you so much that I will not do it without your permission, or if it will damage our friendship."

He responded, "What kind of a question could do that? Please proceed."

I reminded him that during one of our earliest meetings, I had asked to whom he prayed, and I still had questions about that. "Can I raise that again and pursue it more thoroughly?"

He said, "Of course you can."

"Let me start with a scenario of my staying in that apartment you prepared for me on the first floor. I know that you pray several times a day, including at night. To help me understand your idea about prayer, let me ask you some questions. The hour comes in the night that you're supposed to pray; how do you do that? Do you lie in your bed and pray, or do you get up and sit in a chair, or do you dress and go down to the Temple?

He said, "I go down to the Temple."

"Okay, let's still assume that I'm staying in that apartment that you created for me, and I hear your door open and footsteps in the hall. Because we're such good friends, I assume you wouldn't mind if I followed you down to the Temple. When you got there, would you kneel and pray or lie down in a prone position and pray?"

He answered, "I would sit." He showed me that he would be sitting in a lotus position.

"Okay, do you pray silently or out loud?"

"I pray out loud."

"What do you pray about?"

He said, "I pray for my monks and for the nation." We had discussed many times the corruption of several of the Christian pastors as well as the corruption among his monks.

Many of them had taken vows of poverty, but some were getting rich. If a monk asks a Buddhist businessman for a donation, the businessman cannot refuse. Many monks were abusing this and getting rich.

"Now I want to ask again: to whom do you pray?"

"To myself; I am the Buddha."

By the way, he thought I was a Buddha too, a designation I think he assigned to anyone who was very spiritual or who had reached some level of enlightenment.

I continued to probe by asking, "If you are praying to yourself, then you are the one who hears your prayers. Do you have the power to answer your prayers?" At this point, I think he confronted something very deep. It was obviously painful, so I stopped asking questions. My purpose was not to corner him and make him raise a white flag but rather to better understand what he believed.

This report does not end like some missionary letters – with his receiving Jesus and becoming a Baptist. The purpose of these thoughts has simply been to share what took place between a Buddhist monk and me. I have already stated that my goal, from the beginning of our relationship, was not to convert him but rather to be Christ to him. His response was more than I could have imagined. He really liked to talk about Jesus but, of course, never saw him as the son of God or divine. His view of Jesus, both when we began our friendship and during the later stages, was that Jesus was a sage or a wise person like Buddha and Mohammed. They were wise figures of history and were to be listened to. He said that he also loved Jesus, but that his early Christian instruction had probably kept him from thinking about Jesus as I did.

I am fully aware that the following will seem self-aggrandizing, but I must be true to my purpose here and report his response to me. Several times he said, "I sure do like how you talk about Jesus." And another time: "Talking to you must be what it was like to talk to Jesus." My understanding of that statement is that he was feeling loved, maybe for the very first time. I really did love him and remember fondly our times together. He made no confession of faith in Jesus to me, but he has heard the gospel. I do not know what was happening internally, but I pray that, like the thief on the cross, he turned to Jesus before he died. Only Jesus knows whether that happened. Romans 2:16 says, "…on the day of judgment Jesus will judge the secrets of men's hearts…"

Conversations with a Mongolian Doctor

Annually, a joint committee of Congress sponsors the National Prayer Breakfast. From 1969 to 1980, I was the key person for the Middle East; however, in 1980 I became the point person for Asia. One day I received an email from a friend in Japan asking me to invite an acquaintance of his to the Prayer Breakfast.

His friend was Dr. Lkhagwasuren Tserenkhuugyin, who was the director of the Mongolian National University of Medical Science. I initiated contact, and we began a lengthy correspondence about the history and purpose of the Prayer Breakfast. President Eisenhower initiated it in 1953, and annually since that date the President of the United States has been the guest of honor. Of course, at first I couldn't pronounce his name correctly, but soon it was as easy as my own. However, he insisted that I call him Seren, which was his nickname.

I explained that the Prayer Breakfast was held in the Spirit of Jesus. He asked, "Who is he?" When he said that, I remembered an experience that an associate of mine had in Mongolia a few years before I met Seren. It was still an atheistic communist nation and my friend, as a tourist, was assigned a "Government Minder." This Minder was with my friend at all times and noticed that he prayed before meals. Trying not to be obvious, he whispered, "Have you ever felt God?" My friend said yes, and his "Minder" asked, "What did it feel like?" My friend said, "It felt like Jesus." The "Minder" said, "Who is Jesus?" After only a couple of hours of conversation, this man expressed a desire to follow Jesus. I have had the privilege of meeting him many times, and he is now a very serious and committed disciple of Jesus. He and Seren did not know each other but are the same age and grew up in the same culture.

Eventually, Seren agreed to attend the Prayer Breakfast in DC, so we arranged to meet for lunch at the coffee shop of the Washington Hilton. We later learned about his twenty-hour flight (plus three layovers), which God had obviously orchestrated. He flew from Ulaanbaatar to Beijing, but the next leg of his flight experienced a two-day weather delay. Eventually, he traveled from Beijing to San Francisco with another one-day layover, then went on to Minneapolis.

Mary Ann and I departed from Sacramento with a plane change in Minneapolis. When we got on that plane for our flight to DC, she was in the middle seat and I was on the aisle. I looked at the small man in the window seat; he was definitely from Asia. I engaged him in conversation and had not yet asked his name. However, since he was also going to DC, I wondered, 'Could this be Seren?' I asked, "Is your name Dr. Lkhagwasuren Tserenkhuugyin?" He was visibly shocked and asked, "How do you know my name?" He told me later that he thought I might have been from the CIA, which would have been normal back in his country. I then gave him my name and we had a non-stop conversation the rest of the flight. Based on our earlier correspondence, he continued to ask questions about Jesus.

Senator David Durenberger from Minnesota was on our flight, and I recognized him because I had met him several times at the Cedars. We chatted at baggage, and when I said, "We are staying at the Hilton," he offered to give us a ride. Seren told him that we had become unplanned seatmates in Minneapolis: "God was our travel agent and gave us our seats."

We met Seren for lunch on Tuesday. He was blown away by the size of the event and the fact that one hundred sixty-five nations were represented. His questions were always very direct; he wanted to know why Jesus was important to so many people. This led to hours of conversation on the couches in the lobby, in the coffee shop, in our room, and on walks to DuPont Circle. He said that he didn't quite understand everything we talked about but he continued to show enormous interest in Jesus.

We spent Tuesday, Wednesday, and Thursday together, attending the Prayer Breakfast, seminars, and dinners. We also had lots of free time. I was able to answer most of his questions, but the Holy Spirit had not yet done the work of opening his spiritual eyes. I had met with many people like that, so I didn't get frustrated or impatient. However, the intensity of his interest was as strong as any I had experienced.

On Friday morning, we had breakfast in the Hilton coffee shop. I looked up and saw my dear friend Arthur Blessitt and his wife Denise. I called him over and said, "I want to introduce you to my friend, Seren." As you may know, Arthur is the evangelist who has carried the cross in every nation and island group in the world. According to the Guinness Book of Records, he has walked over 42,000 miles carrying the cross and preaching Jesus.

I don't believe it would be an exaggeration to say that within a couple of minutes after I introduced them, Seren was on his knees next to our table, surrendering his life to Jesus. Although he had never heard the name of Jesus until a few months before, the Holy Spirit helped him completely understand the good news about Jesus.

As we had previously planned, he stopped in California to spend a week with us. We had a delightful time that week, and several memories stand out from his stay in our small hometown of Grass Valley.

I will always remember one thing in particular because he must have said it ten to twenty times: "I'm so happy to be in God's family." One evening as my wife prepared dinner, Seren quietly asked me, "Do you tell your wife about Jesus?" When I explained that Mary Ann loved Jesus as much as I did, he said, "Oh wonderful, I will tell my wife she needs Jesus in her heart." A few minutes later, he asked, "Do you tell children about Jesus"? I told him that my two girls had been raised from an early age to understand the good news about Jesus and that they had each decided to be His disciple.

He said, "I can't wait to tell my children what has happened to me and that they can also be part of God's family."

As we took him to the airport, Seren told us that his heart was filled with joy and that he had a strong resolve to help his family and the medical community understand how to have Jesus in their hearts.

Wikipedia reports that in 1989 there were only four Christians in Mongolia. Today there are more than 50,000, with evangelicals growing the fastest. I don't know for sure, but my guess is that Seren is a big part of that.

Conversation on the Subway

I've calculated that in thirty-plus years, I drove to San Francisco at least eight hundred and fifty times. Every other week for three days, I was in the financial district, meeting with individuals and a number of groups. I stayed with close friends in the suburbs; it amazes me even now to think that during all those years, I rode the subway into the city only one time. That one subway ride produced the following conversation.

At the end of a very long day, I got on BART at the Montgomery Street station to ride back under the bay to the Oakland Hills. The car was jam-packed, with standing room only. It was so full that it was impossible to not be touching someone. I happened to be standing next to a very nice Japanese businessman who was holding a briefcase because there was not enough room for him to set it on the floor. I said, "Let me move over a little so you can set that down." This allowed him to set his briefcase between his legs and mine. We exchanged greetings, and because we had about a forty-five-minute ride, I asked, "Where are you going to get off?"

Lafayette, he told me. I said, "I'll get off at Orinda." He asked if I commuted every day.

"No, this is the first time I've ever ridden BART."

He was surprised. "Don't you work in the city?"

"No, I come here for only a few days every other week."

He asked what my business was and why I came to San Francisco. I think my answer was something like, "I come to visit my friend Walter Hoadley and a number of other men."

He said, "I've met him a couple of times at banking conferences, because I'm a manager of a bank in San Francisco." He had followed Walter's career, so he knew that Walter had been President of the Federal Reserve Bank in Philadelphia and economic advisor to the President, and that he was currently executive vice president and chief economist for Bank of America. I told the man that for several years I had met monthly with Walter and a group of other men at the Bankers Club on the top floor of the Bank of America building.

He asked, "What kind of group is it?"

"It's a group in which we have fellowship in Jesus. Each month, a different person shares his spiritual journey." I told him that I thought he would enjoy it and said, "On one of my future visits, I will stop by your office and we can discuss it further."

He said, "I'd like that," so we exchanged business cards. We talked about a number of other things and lost track of time; suddenly it was time for me to get off at my stop.

Now the irony of this story begins. In some ways, it was just another casual conversation with a stranger on the subway, a stranger I would probably never see again. But I had taken his card and made a commitment that I would visit him someday. Yet three months later, I had forgotten about him. One day I remembered our conversation and started looking for his card but couldn't find it. I looked in the pockets of all my suits and around my desk, but it was not to be found. I felt a twinge of conscience and realized that I should try to find him.

I remembered that he was the manager of a bank, so during my next trip to San Francisco I decided to track him down. Unfortunately, I had forgotten his name and even the name of his bank. Numerous banks are in the financial district of San Francisco, so on each successive trip, I went to at least two banks, asking if they had a Japanese manager in their system. Eventually, I had gone to fifteen banks asking that question. About five months after we had met, a bank employee finally told me, "Yes, the manager of their main branch at Montgomery and Pine is Japanese."

I immediately went to that location, which was one of the big, international banks. The office was large – actually, it was half a block deep. As I opened the front door, I could see all the way to the back of the room, where the executive offices were located. His office had a glass wall, and I could see him sitting at his desk. I recognized him immediately, and for some reason, he looked up at that moment and saw me. The entire time I walked toward him, he watched me. I entered his office and had not yet spoken when he picked up my card from his desk, looked at it, looked at me, and said, "I wondered if you would ever come." That man was Art Mitsutome and what started as a conversation between two strangers on the subway developed into a wonderfully warm friendship. I have stayed in his home several times and have enjoyed numerous meals with him.

Now for a very condensed account of the months that followed our meeting at his office. Art became a regular at our Bank of America prayer breakfast, met Jesus, was baptized, and led his wife, Anne, to Christ. In the process of getting to know Art, I learned that he had been raised a Buddhist. Art told me that before he gave his life to Jesus, his entire family tree had contained only one non-Buddhist. The only follower of Jesus in six generations of Buddhists was his cousin Doug Muraki. When Art told me that, I was speechless because Doug Muraki was the pastor of my daughter's church in Sacramento. Oh, how I love serendipities!

Art and Anne became very active in the Japanese church where they were baptized. That church was affiliated with JEMS (Japanese Evangelical Missionary Society), and Art eventually became a state leader of that organization.

Art and Anne planned, promoted, and executed a couples retreat for Bank of America men's group. About fifty couples attended the very successful retreat at the Mt. Hermon conference center in the Santa Cruz Mountains.

Art's love of the Scriptures led him to gravitate toward the international ministry of the Gideons. Some of you may not know the Gideons; they are the people who place Bibles in hotel rooms and encourage the reading of the Bible. Eventually, Art took on the responsibility of leading that organization for Northern California while remaining in the investment firm he founded.

Thank you, Jesus, for overcrowded subway cars.

Conversation with
the President of a Technology Company

On a flight home from Colorado, I noticed an ad in a technology magazine. It was promoting a product that was new to me. I am an early adopter, so I was interested in this new technology. I noticed that the company was in the industrial park I would be visiting for an upcoming appointment with the president of Sega. Though the address was not a retail location, I decided to drop by, and try to get a look at this product. I liked what I saw, but God had another reason for my visiting that company. He had made an appointment for me that was not on my calendar.

When I arrived, the receptionist greeted me. I explained that their advertisement in Wired magazine had piqued my interest. "I know this is a distribution warehouse, not retail sales, but since I was in the neighborhood, I was hoping to see it."

She was very gracious and said, "It would normally be available to see, but all the salespeople are in Las Vegas at Comdex, the computer trade show."

I showed a bit of disappointment and said, "Oh, that's too bad. I won't be here again for a month or so."

As I mentioned, she was very gracious (and I'm certain was prompted by God) and volunteered, "The President is here; maybe he will show it to you." She spoke to him on the phone, and shortly he came to the reception area.

He was a tall, slim Korean in his mid-thirties, with a strong accent. He was not very talkative until I said that I had recently returned from ten days in Seoul.

He asked the reason for my visit. I replied, "To spend time with my friends who are in the government." I told him that I had been to Seoul more than forty times and had many good friends there. That really sparked his interest, so I intentionally started to drop the names of my friends. I mentioned the last five presidents and their cabinets, numerous senior people in the business world, plus Gi Kwang, the Chief Buddhist Monk of Korea.

He was visibly shocked and asked, "Why do you meet with them? Are you with the U.S. government?" When I said no, he asked, "Are you a businessman?"

I said, "No, I have no agenda except friendship. Now, after many years, these friends trust me and believe that to be true." I told him how much I had come to love Korea and that my long-term hope was that someday the nation would have leaders who were led by God, not by their own self-interest.

At that point, he stared directly into my eyes without speaking for several uncomfortable seconds. It was an extremely dramatic moment. Later, I told my wife that it was so unusual, it seemed like the lights had gone off, or if they were off, they had just turned on.

When he finally spoke, he said, "You look like a man I can trust. I've lost my way. Can you help me?"

Those were his exact words, and they stunned me. I said, "Wow, that's a heavy statement. Can you give me a paragraph on what it means to lose your way?"

I knew he wouldn't want to have this conversation in front of the receptionist, so I suggested that we continue in his office. After we got there, I said, "Before we talk about this, why don't you tell me a bit about your life's journey?" The following is a very condensed version of the story he told me.

He was an only child born in Seoul to parents who were both doctors. They sent him to the best schools and later to Seoul National University, the Harvard of Korea. His major was computer engineering; then he went to Stanford University to get his masters. While he was still a student there, he started a company that did so well, the newspapers and magazines in Seoul wrote stories about the local boy who had hit it big in Silicon Valley. Later, a prestigious Korean technology company offered him a position. Now he was president of that company's U.S. division. His aunt found the perfect wife for him, and they had a son. My experience in Korea helped me understand what a big deal that was for a Korean man. As he talked, he said, "I've lost my way" four different times. He did not use the following words, but the sentiment I was picking up was, "I have achieved everything I wanted to do and I thought it would bring me meaning, but I feel unfulfilled." I think his statement "I've lost my way" was his way of saying, "Is that all there is?"

I told him that I had some thoughts about what he was experiencing. He said, "Please continue." I said, "Let me start by saying that God made us in His image."

He interrupted and said, "I don't believe in God. I'm Buddhist."

Based on Scripture and many personal experiences, I knew that while men could be atheistic in their philosophy, they all had a God-given inner awareness of a power greater than themselves. I wanted to speak to that part of him.

I said, "That's okay, you don't have to believe in God. I do, and you asked at the reception desk, 'Can you help me?' I don't know if I can help you, but I have an idea for you to consider." I continued: "God created us in His image and gave us free will and the ability to understand right from wrong. He also made us triune beings, so each of us has a body, soul, and Spirit. It looks like you have taken very good care of your body; you probably have a personal trainer."

He said, "I do, and I was with him this morning."

"Now, regarding your soul, which consists of your mind, will, and emotions. You have done an excellent job of training your mind in technology and management. Your emotions seem to be under control, and your will has helped you make some good decisions.

"You have paid a lot of attention to your body and soul, but I think you have neglected your spirit, which is the most critical part of your being. Can I talk with you about that?

He said, "Yes, I want to hear whatever you have to say."

I offered a short version of the story of the Garden of Eden and how God had created the human race with a spirit that was alive and connected to Him. "However, our grandparents, Adam and Eve, decided they wanted to be their own God. When they acted on this, they became disconnected from the life of God, and their spirits died. This meant all their descendants would also have a dead spirit. All means all, so that includes you and me.

"Let me give you an analogy of what it means to have a dead spirit. Think of a car without gas. It's still a car, but it's lifeless without the power source that can make it work correctly. In the same way, humans without the life force of God's Spirit are still humans but are spiritually dead." I suggested that his feeling of having lost his way was God's method of alerting him to the fact that his spirit was on empty. I asked if I could talk to him about Jesus.

Again, he said, "Yes, of course," but this time he seemed eager to hear what I had to say.

I explained the incarnation of Jesus and His work on our behalf. This man melted before my eyes. When I asked if he wanted to have his spirit made new, he said yes. That day he asked Jesus to be his savior, and his spirit became alive to God.

Postscript

About two weeks later, I was visiting him and it was as if I were speaking to a different person. I brought him the Bible on CD, which he now listens to during his forty-five-minute commute. As we talked, he shared that recently he had done something very strange. During our first visit, he hadn't told me that even though he had a wife and a son; he also had a mistress. He had given her a credit card, a Mercedes, and an apartment. He said he didn't understand why he'd done it, but he told her that he wouldn't be coming to see her anymore. She could keep the apartment, car, and credit card for six months; then it would end and she would have to make other arrangements. I explained that this was the Holy Spirit helping him have a life that pleased God.

During another visit, he said that his wife did not understand his attempts to explain God to her. He asked if I would meet with her. I agreed, so he chose a famous Chinese restaurant on the Embarcadero in San Francisco. He brought his wife and mother-in-law, who lived with them. He didn't allow much time for small talk; he wanted me to explain God to them before we even ordered. It was a bit uncomfortable, but I tried to repeat what I had told him during our first meeting. They listened but seemed uninterested; however, they said they were happy for him. He got mad at them and said, "You aren't even trying to understand." Later, I explained to him that if I had come to his office a week before I did, he likely would not have been receptive. I told him that he should pray for them and it would happen in God's timing. That evening, his wife did agree to put their child in a Christian school so he could learn about God.

This encounter is a wonderful story but it's only the visible part of his story. The unseen parts are the months and maybe years that God had been preparing this man's heart for that encounter. That's what allowed a man to move from atheist to believer in a couple of hours.

This man is an example of the multitudes of people who are searching for meaning and purpose in life. Most of them are unaware that they can find it in Jesus alone.

Conversations with a Korean Congressman

As some of you know, over the last thirty-six years, I have been to Seoul, Korea fifty-five times. Often, I am asked, "What caused you to have an interest in Korea?" I thought I would give a brief account of how that happened.

I believe it was in late 1979 that Doug Coe, my good friend and associate, called with a request. He told me that he had promised to speak at the Korean Presidential Prayer Breakfast but for medical reasons was unable to travel. He asked if I would go in his place. I told him that I had no interest in Asia. At that time, I was the Middle East point person for the Congressional Committee that sponsored our National Prayer Breakfast. I had built strong relationships with leaders in many of those countries. However, Doug was very persuasive, and eventually I agreed to go. I told him it would be only one time; then I would return to my focus on Middle East relationships.

That first visit was for ten days in February of 1980. Doug had given me the names of several senior leaders, who welcomed me with open arms and treated me royally (embarrassingly so). This was probably because Doug had sent a letter of introduction, signed by two Senators and two

Congressmen. I had a wonderful time meeting a few business executives; however, during that first visit, most of my contacts were elected officials. Of course, I also met many new people who had no connection to our U.S. Presidential Prayer Breakfast. One of them was Congressman Kim, Chai Ho, who represented the southeast coast of Korea and was the former mayor of Yeosu. I was told that he was known as the "Mr. Clean" of Korean politics. He spoke broken English, but we seemed to get along just fine. It must have been God-ordained because, without planning it, we spent a lot of time together. We became good friends, and he had a very helpful attitude. He introduced me to Prime Minister Yoo, Chang-Soon and also President Chun, Doo-Hwan, and later the six presidents who followed him. However, at that time, I was still sure that this would be a one-time experience.

Congressman Kim and others had taken me to Seoul's finest restaurants. On my last evening in Seoul, he asked if he could take me to dinner again. My guess was that he was planning one more of those very expensive restaurants. I agreed on the condition that he take me to his favorite restaurant, one that he frequented when he was not entertaining a guest. I said, "One where they know you because you eat there often." It took a little persuasion, but he finally agreed. It turned out that his favorite was a small Korean restaurant with only about six tables but excellent Korean home cooking. At first, he was apologetic about the ambiance, but when I assured him that I liked it, he loosened up. After that, we had a very special evening with lots of conversation about our families and personal lives.

At the end of our dinner, I asked him if he knew of a high place where we could have a cup of coffee and see the lights of the city. He quickly said, "Yes, that would be the Bugak Sky House on Bugak Mountain." He called his driver, and it took us about an hour to get to the top of the mountain. I was surprised to see a very nice three-story round restaurant that was a favorite place for young people to take their dates. We went to the top floor and had ice cream and a cup of coffee. Afterward, we went out on the wide circular deck that surrounded the restaurant. By walking around the building, we could see the entire city. I don't know what the population was at that time, but today the metro area of Seoul contains twenty-six million people and is one of the largest cities in the world. From our vantage point, I think we could see the lights of the entire area.

I had learned that Congressman Kim was Presbyterian, so as we looked at the city, I asked him if he had ever prayed with his eyes open. He said no, so I told him that it was my habit to find a high place and pray for every country I visited. I reminded him that Jesus looked on Jerusalem from the high vantage point of the Mount of Olives and wept over its spiritual condition. I told him we could talk to God out loud with our eyes open and people would just think we were talking to each other. He said, "Ok, you pray."

I began praying for the area and saw a bridge in the distance. I remembered that a few days earlier, I had been under that bridge where four hundred homeless people lived. Below us and to my right was the area where their "White House" was located. They call theirs the "Blue House" because it's a very large residence and has a distinctive Asian blue tile roof. The Korean name is Cheong wa dae. I prayed for the President of Korea, whom I had visited a few days earlier. After a few minutes of prayer for the nation, I stopped and waited for Congressman Kim to pray, but he quickly disappeared back inside the restaurant. I thought I might have embarrassed or offended him, but shortly he returned with a photographer who had a Polaroid camera. He instructed the photographer to take our picture standing at the rail. After we had received two copies of the picture (I still have my copy), we started down to the limousine. When we got into the back seat, Congressman Kim told his driver to remain parked, then turned to me. He was very sober and said, "Glenn, when we are in public you should call me Congressman Kim, but when we have private time, please call me Chai Ho." I had done some research on Asian culture, so I knew that though he was a couple years older than I was, he had just invited me to have an elder brother relationship with him. He was really old school, and during a subsequent visit, I learned that his wife Sook-Ja didn't even call him by his first name. She may have had endearing names for him, but only his father and elder brother addressed him by his first name. Therefore, he had given me a special, very rare gift.

The next day, he took me to the airport and arranged for us to spend two hours in the airline lounge. There, we continued to cement our relationship. On the flight home, I had a thought pattern develop that seemed very real at the time. Later I told my wife, "I think while I was praying for Korea on Bugak Mountain, God opened my shirt and slipped Korea into my heart. It was actually a surprise to me that I developed a serious love for the people of Korea. I'm quite sure that I will be going back again." I didn't realize it would be again and again and again.

Over the ensuing years, Chai Ho became my closest friend in Korea and opened a number of doors for me. One example was Kang, Sung-Mo, who was president and CEO of the Korean equivalent of General Electric. We became great friends, and Mr. Kang volunteered to provide me with a hotel, car, and driver for every one of my trips to Korea. When I politely declined, he told me that I would be robbing him of the joy of enabling my ministry to the leaders of his country. I accepted, and he continued to do this for over thirty years. He wanted nothing in return but a dinner with me during each visit. It was a joy to accommodate his request because he was such a wonderful friend.

I thank God for Kim, Chai Ho, who has been such a great ministry partner and faithful friend. I helped him get his children into a private high school in Berkeley, and now his four children call me Uncle Glenn. We have traveled to

China, Japan, Hong Kong, and the United States together, as well as to several retreats. I was able to return his many favors by arranging for him to have his picture taken with President Bush. He said that was the highlight of his life.

We are both getting older, and only the Lord knows what He has in store for us. We do know, however, that we will spend eternity together with Jesus.

That is a bit of the story of why I love Korea and why it's like a second home to me.

Conversation with a Dying Man

One of my closest friends in San Francisco was Frank Haas, who was in a local TEC group. TEC is the acronym for 'The Executive Committee,' an international business consulting company. Each group consists of twelve CEOs or company presidents and acts as a business roundtable to help its members. It is led by a TEC Chairman, who is the facilitator, coach, and advisor.

For many years, Don Cope was the TEC Chairman of Frank's group. Frank had been open about his faith, but he and Don had never spoken about it in depth. One day Don called Frank and asked for a private meeting during which he told Frank that his doctor had given him some bad news. Don had stage four cancer that had metastasized throughout his body. He was unlikely to live more than a few months. Don did not have a spiritual background, but the reason he called Frank was to talk with him about Jesus. Frank explained the gospel to Don, who was eager to embrace it. That day, they prayed together and Don put his faith in Jesus.

That same afternoon, Frank called me to tell me that Don was our new brother in Christ. He asked if I would meet with him. I had met Don only once but had enjoyed our time together, so I quickly agreed. Frank said, "I knew you would say yes so I already told him you would be calling."

When I called Don the first time, he was so warm and friendly that we chatted for over an hour. During our first face-to-face meeting, he said that Frank had told him I could help him get ready to meet Jesus. Don said, "I know practically nothing about the Bible, and I don't want to be embarrassed when I meet Jesus." He was very sincere about this and asked, "Can you help me be the best disciple I can be in the time I have left?" I did not feel led to fill his head with doctrine but to simply feed his hunger for a more intimate heart connection with Jesus. Of course, we covered lots of Scripture, but it was always in response to what I sensed God was doing in Don's heart.

Only a month after we started meeting, Don became bedridden. Though his mind remained sharp, I watched him quickly lose weight and muscle tone. It was the very definition of bittersweet: painful to watch his body failing while rejoicing as he grew stronger spiritually. He loved the Scriptures, and his prayers were both simple and sweet but as profound as any I had ever heard. I was there to encourage him, but I was the one who was being deeply encouraged.

A month before he died, Don said to me, "I don't know any pastors, so would you speak at my memorial?" He said he wanted it to be at Trader Vic's, his favorite waterfront restaurant on the San Francisco Bay. He loved having lunch or sunset dinners there while watching the windsurfers. He was a very organized man and had written instructions about his desires for his memorial. His plans included what he wanted me to say because most of the attendees would be non-believers. He wanted me to give them the details of his conversion. He said, "Don't make it the short version. Make it as if I were telling them myself because I know these folks and they need to hear about Jesus."

We met at 2:30 in the afternoon, and as Don had hoped, the windsurfers were out in good numbers. Many people loved Don, but he invited only his closest friends. Still, two hundred people attended, with some flying in from Europe and Asia. Don had asked a few others to say a few words and most of them spoke of how much they had learned from him. One person was quite humorous and told some funny stories about Don's college life. It was a solemn time but also joyous and a real celebration of Don's life.

I honored Don's request and told the group the intimate story of his belated love of Jesus. "He wanted you to know that he died with peace in his heart because he was certain that he would spend eternity with Jesus in heaven." I gave them some first-person statements from Don, like: "I know this will come as a shock that I have become a Jesus person, but it is so real and meaningful to me that I wanted Glenn to tell you about it."

After the service, several people wanted to talk to me, so we chatted for a few minutes. One of them had a desire for a deeper dialogue, so we arranged to have lunch. He was the dean of admissions at one of the top universities in the Bay Area. He had a multitude of questions about God but was so moved by Don's testimony that a month after our first lunch he gave his life to Jesus. I asked him if he knew of other believers at the university. He did, so we formed a small weekly fellowship group in his office.

A second man at that memorial service was Don's longtime friend and a real estate investor. He owned real estate all over the Bay Area and even had several properties in my hometown of Grass Valley. We spent many hours discussing why he hated the church so much. We finally discovered the seat of his bitterness, and after he surrendered his life to Jesus, he was able to move past it. He was Armenian, and as a child had suffered sexual abuse at the hands of a priest in his Orthodox church. Because he was a friend of the man at the university, he joined the fellowship group that met in his office.

Other connections were made during that time, but I simply wanted to relate my conversations with a man who came to faith late in his life. This was so much more than a deathbed conversion; the Holy Spirit caused him to fall in love with Jesus. I wish more believers had the genuineness and joy of Don's faith. He also left a tremendous legacy for his friends. Two of them (whom we know about) became followers of Jesus, but only God knows how the others responded to Don's testimony.

As I reflect on those days, I consider it a wonderful gift that the Lord allowed me to spend time with Don during the last four months of his life. God was definitely glorified by the life of Don Cope.

Conversation with a Friend
Who Doesn't Believe in God

While meeting with the CEO of an oil company in San Francisco, I got into a discussion about the current political atmosphere in our nation. He was especially concerned about the progressive versus conservative differences but went on to include other categories. Eventually, the discussion turned to the general topic of freedom and democracy, and our views were pretty much in sync. I asked him who he thought had made the greatest contribution to freedom worldwide. He thought that Ronald Reagan and Margaret Thatcher should be considered because of their roles in the breakup of the Soviet Union. That event led to the overthrow of several dictators in Eastern Europe, giving millions their freedom. I agreed with him and added Abraham Lincoln and Martin Luther King, Jr. Then I said, "I was thinking on a grander scale, in which case my choice would be Jesus." When he didn't verbally object, I continued.

I said, "An honest review of history will show that with very few exceptions, human freedom has flourished where Jesus is honored. The reverse is also true; wherever the gospel of Jesus has been prohibited, people have been enslaved and millions have died. Prime examples are the atheistic nations of Russia, China, and North Korea. However, even in those countries and others around the globe, Jesus motivates His followers to establish hospitals, orphanages, schools, agricultural and clean water projects, etc." I went on to say that, in my opinion, if Jesus were only human, He would deserve more attention than any other person who ever lived.

When he said, "That's probably true," I responded, "Then why don't you become a follower of Jesus?" He seemed a little shocked by the question and said, "That's impossible! You know I don't believe in God."

I replied, "Most Christians would agree with you that it's impossible to follow Jesus without believing in God. But since I personally know a number of non-believers who are following Jesus, I wouldn't let that stop you." He, like many who will read this, was skeptical. Therefore, I will try to explain why I have this kind of interaction with agnostics and atheists.

I told him about the huge crowds that followed Jesus, sometimes numbering into the thousands. When Jesus moved from place to place, they followed Him. When He got into a boat and crossed the lake, they followed Him. Then I asked, "Using Biblical terms, do you think they were all born-again believers"? The obvious answer is no; the Bible confirms this when it describes numerous scenarios of His interaction with individual followers.

The definitive answer comes from the Apostle Mark: "While Jesus was having dinner at Levi's house, *many tax collectors and 'sinners'* were eating with him and his disciples, for there were many who followed him." (Mk 2:15) Let me restate that: *many tax collectors and sinners were followers of Jesus.* Most Christians think that only born-again believers can be followers of Jesus, so how can we reconcile this dilemma? The answer is that there are actually two ways of following Jesus.

The first is an external following like the crowds that followed Jesus. Some wanted to be healed; some liked His teachings, and some were merely curious, staying in the back of the crowd, hoping no one would recognize them. However, it's obvious that everyone following Him had some level of interest, however small.

Therefore, when I'm meeting with a person who has a negative view of Jesus as the Son of God, my approach is to encourage them to develop some level of interest about the historical Jesus. There was much more to the conversation with my atheist friend mentioned in the first paragraph, but he did say, "I agree that I probably should know a little more about the historical Jesus." Because he seemed open to that idea, I told him that Jesus had a best friend who had written a book about Him. I suggested that reading that book would be a good place to start. When he asked for the name of Jesus' best friend, I told him it was John. My friend knew immediately whom I was talking about, but he was still non-committal. However, during a subsequent conversation, he raised the subject: "I've been reading a bit about the life of Jesus." This is often the way people become external followers of Jesus.

The second way to follow Jesus is an internal following. People who follow Jesus externally for some period of time usually receive an opportunity to respond to Jesus' invitation to exchange their life for His life. If they decide to receive His life, and therefore salvation, the following verse becomes a reality for them: "The one, who has been with you, shall be in you." (Jn 14:17 NIV) The Bible says that this person is Born Again, Saved, Regenerate, In Christ and becomes a New Creation. Each person has his or her own unique experience with Jesus because He was personal with every individual during His days on earth. The same is true today.

I wish this were true for all my friends, but many freely express their disbelief in God. Therefore, I try to relate to them in the same way that Philip responded to his friend when he didn't believe Jesus was the Messiah. Phillip was one of the first disciples of Jesus and wanted his friend Nathaniel to become one as well. However, when Nathaniel expressed a negative attitude toward Jesus, Phillip didn't try to use logic to convince him. He simply said, "Come and see for yourself." (John 1:46 NLT) You know the rest of the story. Nathanael went to see for himself and ended up becoming a disciple of Jesus. In that same spirit, I encourage nonbelievers to "come and see" by following the historical Jesus. While He had unwavering requirements for

His disciples (Luke 14:25-27, 33), He had no preconditions for followers.

Even among those who *do* believe there is a God, I find this approach useful at times because most of them are not followers of Jesus. As we spend time together, I usually learn their view about issues of faith. While many have a negative view of churches or overly zealous Christians, most have quite a positive opinion of Jesus. That has been my experience when I meet with numerous people of the Islamic faith in the Middle East. They claim that Jesus was a great prophet, "but not the son of God." Rather than debating His divinity, I agree with them that He was a great prophet and simply ask, "What are some of His prophesies that you like?" They usually don't know any. I tell them it would be consistent with their belief to know more about what He said.

When meeting with Jewish friends or others who think He was a good teacher (Rabbi), I ask, "What are your favorite things he taught?" Surprisingly, they typically can't think of anything. Therefore, because they already think he was a teacher, I start there and try to encourage a curiosity about what he taught. Only the Holy Spirit can open a person's eyes, and I'm convinced that if they genuinely follow the historical Jesus, they will eventually encounter the same Jesus I know. Actually, the only Jesus anyone can follow is the one in whom they currently believe. That is true of even the most mature believer. I know for a fact that I have a more definitive picture of Jesus now than I did when I started following Him fifty-seven years ago.

When the Holy Spirit prompts me, I always make it clear to external followers of Jesus that it's a pre-salvation journey. Eventually, and at just the right time, God will lead you to the cross; He always does. The cross is an instrument of death, so He will make it clear to you that He is inviting you to die to self and receive His eternal life. If you decide to do that, you become a follower of an internal Jesus.

You might ask, "Is there is a place for preaching about sin, judgment, heaven, and hell?" My answer is a definite *yes*. However, recognize that when people respond, it's because they have been external followers of Jesus for some time. This is what I am trying to get believers to understand and to encourage among their unbelieving friends. Paul was actively against Jesus but had a sudden, miraculous conversion on the road to Damascus. We must recognize that he is the exception, not the norm, as most individuals have a much less dramatic conversion.

For most of us, Peter is the example. When Jesus asked Peter to follow Him, did He say, "Now, before you park your boat, do you believe that I was virgin born and that I'm the Messiah?" The answer is *no*; He just said to Peter, "Follow me." And Peter did, but this teacher was much more than he knew at the time. Eventually, Jesus asked him, "Who do you say I am?" While Peter was following Jesus externally, God opened his eyes and he could answer,

"You are the Christ (Messiah)." In response, Jesus told him, "My Father in Heaven revealed that to you." (Mat. 16:15-17 NIV)

It's the same for people today. We can encourage them to follow the historical Jesus, but only God the Father can open their eyes to the true nature of Jesus. Why do we insist that people believe what we believe before they can start following Jesus? Jesus didn't.

Conversations with a Buddhist Legislator

In Seoul, a friend of many years asked me to meet one of his childhood friends. At this point, both were in their mid to late sixties, and each was a very senior Korean government official. My friend was in the president's cabinet, and his friend was a legislator, committee chairman, and political party leader. My friend was an evangelical follower of Jesus, and the man he wanted me to meet was a practicing Buddhist. They had maintained their friendship for almost sixty years – a Korean quality that I admire immensely.

An appointment was set up, and I was told that we had fifteen minutes. To honor the confidentiality of our relationship, I will refer to this man as Hyun Oh. My friend introduced me as a completely apolitical person and a man he could trust. Because they completely trusted each other, this was a ringing endorsement.

After a few minutes of small talk, we transitioned to more substantive topics. Because Hyun Oh was an expert in national intelligence, I asked him what his greatest concern was for the nation. He was very open and explained a difficult situation with North Korea. I am certain that he did not give me any information that I could not find on my own, but it seemed like he was being very vulnerable. As we were nearing the end of our very short meeting, I asked if it would be all right if I prayed for him. I thought his answer was no, so I stood up to leave. He said, "Aren't you going to pray?" I explained that I had misunderstood his answer and then I sat back down. I prayed a very short prayer for him and the issue we had discussed. Then, keeping our commitment, we left after a fifteen-minute meeting.

Later that evening, I received a phone call in my hotel room from Hyun Oh's chief of staff. He said the congressman wanted to meet with me the next morning for breakfast. I accepted and agreed to meet him in the lobby at 7:30 am. Though I'd already had a breakfast scheduled, I knew that it could be rescheduled, and I sensed that breakfast with Hyun Oh was where God was leading me.

He was right on time, which told me that our meeting was important to him, as morning traffic in Seoul is horrendous. I quickly recognized him, and He told me that because this was a last-minute meeting, every private dining room in the hotel was unavailable. (By the way, it was a hotel with twenty-three restaurants.) I said, "That's not a problem for me. Let's eat in one of the coffee shops." He said he would prefer a private room, so he had arranged for us to have a table in the ballroom, which seated several thousand people. This meant we had one small table in the corner of an immense, empty ballroom. It was a very unusual setting but, looking back, I realize it became a special memory for both of us.

As we sat down, Hyun Oh opened the conversation by telling me how meaningful my prayer had been to him. Almost verbatim, he recounted every word I had said. He told me that he was under an immense amount of pressure, and my prayer had been a real encouragement to him. Later, I learned more about the stress he was speaking about. Then we continued the conversation that had begun in his office, and he shared more details about the North Korean problem. I got the impression that these things were not public knowledge. As I reflect on that morning, I believe God used that breakfast to bond our hearts in friendship.

We began our relationship during a period of political unrest in Korea. It was a time marked by political, labor, student, and farmer protests that often turned violent. On one occasion, the rioters detonated a bomb across the street from my hotel, severely damaging the American Consulate. At times, hundreds of thousands of people were in the streets, and the police and military were everywhere. More than once, while returning to my hotel, I experienced the uncomfortable effect of drifting tear gas. Every day the TV and newspapers reported criminal allegations against many politicians. From the newspapers, I learned that Hyun Oh was facing charges that were quite serious. As best I could discern, they were trumped up, but they were serious enough that, if proven, he faced the possibility of imprisonment. I think this was what motivated my friend to introduce me to Hyun Oh.

One time I met him in his office when he was quite depressed and feeling very alone in the world. I prayed with him and said, "Hyun Oh, I am your friend and I will be there for you whether you go to prison or become president." That was so meaningful to him that later he said several times publicly, "Every person should have one essential friend like Glenn Murray." The political intrigue eventually ended with several people going to jail, but Hyun Oh was exonerated.

We continued to meet, and because we really enjoyed each other, we had many private dinners with late-night discussions. I speak about Jesus easily and naturally, so I often wondered why I felt a check about engaging him in a serious discussion of the gospel. He and I often talked about Jesus, but it was generic in nature, or about my own faith in Christ. I was waiting for the Spirit to prompt me to pursue a deeper dialogue with Hyun Oh.

When that moment finally arrived, we were having lunch alone in a private room at his men's club. Ten minutes after we sat down, I felt what I had been waiting for. It was what I have come to call the prompting of the Holy Spirit. Before I share what happened that day, I believe a little background on Buddhism would help you understand the context of our discussion. Regarding God, Buddhism claims to be agnostic; however, practically it works out to be atheism. Buddha said, "It is impossible to know whether or not there is a God, so forget about the question." That meant my friend Hyun Oh had been raised in a system of thought that denied the existence of God. He though he didn't believe in God, but I felt that deep inside he had to be aware of something greater than himself. I wanted to pursue that based on several Scriptures that are central to my thinking when I meet with atheists or Buddhists.

The Apostle Paul states *"…what can be known about God is plain to them, because God has shown it to them."* (Rom, 1: 19-20) The Old Testament supports that in the following verse: *"…God has planted eternity in the human heart…"* (Ec 3:11) Another New Testament verse says, *"…In the past he permitted all the nations to go their own ways, but he never left them without evidence of himself and his goodness."* (Acts 14:16-17 NLT) This means that every person on earth cannot avoid having an innate sense of something greater than themselves. I look for that in every person I meet, but I wait for God's direction in how to proceed. With Hyun Oh, I had waited far longer than normal but now I definitely felt the Holy Spirit prompting me, so I took the direct approach.

I asked him if I could ask a personal question. He was a little annoyed with me and said, "Of course, but I don't know why you would ask me for permission. I thought our friendship allowed us to ask personal questions of one another." I apologized and said, "That's true, but this question is sensitive because it is about your religion." He said, "No problem. What do you want to know?"

Rather than confronting his belief system, the Lord gave me a question that was intentionally designed to bypass it. "Have you ever been in a difficult situation that made you feel like you had to talk to God or that God was trying to talk to you?" He took my question seriously and thought deeply for several seconds. Then he answered, "Yes, I think twice. Once when I was a child and once during the Korean War." My response was, "I felt very comfortable asking you that question because the Bible says that every person on earth has had that experience."

Then I asked if he knew anything about Blaise Pascal, the sixteenth-century French mathematician and physicist. He did know a little about him, so I gave Hyun Oh a famous quote attributed to Pascal: *"There is a God-shaped vacuum in the heart of every person, and it can never be filled by any created thing. It can only be filled by God, made known through Jesus Christ."* I added my editorial comments and explained that a vacuum abhors a vacuum and longs to be filled. Down through the centuries, men have tried to fill that vacuum with power, possessions, pleasure, etc., but because it is in the shape of God, only God can fill that hole in our hearts.

While explaining the God-shaped vacuum, I kept pointing at my heart with my index finger. I must have given him the impression that it is a very small area in every man. He was quiet for a few moments. Then, as if something might be wrong with him, he said, "Glenn, I think I have a very big one." I affirmed what he was feeling and told him that I had the same feeling when I discovered the hole in my heart. However, when I surrendered my life to Jesus, He forgave all my sins, filled that hole in my heart, and gave me peace with God.

This led to many questions and a fuller explanation of the gospel. After about thirty minutes, Hyun Oh said, "I would like Jesus to forgive my sins and give me eternal life." We prayed together, and the power of the Holy Spirit was evident as he went from death to life and from an atheist to a brother in Christ. Hyun Oh now attends a weekly Bible study with a few men, and I'm encouraged by his spiritual growth.

I am so glad I waited for God's timing. If I had pushed Hyun Oh before the right moment, he would not have been ready and may have been driven away. This experience helped me fully understand that God's timing is perfect. It also helped me with numerous future relationships.

Conversation That Changed
the Direction of My Life!

In 1964, I received a phone call from a missionary who was home on furlough from Taiwan. We knew each other because my church supported him, so he called with a request. It was eleven o'clock at night, so he apologized but said he didn't know who else to call. His dilemma was that he was scheduled to speak to a group of men the next morning but was very ill with the flu. I wasn't keen on doing it but agreed to speak in his place. I asked about the size, makeup, and location of the group. He said it would be sixty men, half of whom were unbelievers. At the time, this was right in my sweet spot, so I perked up immediately. I was very active with Campus Crusade for Christ, led a large Young Life Club at Del Campo High School, and was being discipled by Marv Ladner, a longtime member of the Navigator staff. Therefore, evangelism/discipleship was a major focus of my life.

I showed up the next morning and gave a salvation message, with an emphasis on the cross. As I reflect back on that morning, I believe some might have said that I backed up my gospel dump truck and dumped the whole load. I don't know if I used the term "turn or burn," but I probably painted a very vivid picture of what would happen to un-believers who died without receiving Jesus. Heaven or hell was the choice and today was the day to decide. I asked for a show of hands of who wanted to receive Jesus. I probably felt good about my presentation.

Afterward, I spoke with a few people. When most had left, an older gentleman (he was fifty-three, I was twenty-seven) approached and asked if he could walk me to my car. His name was Dick Barram, and we stood by my car and talked for more than an hour. He seemed to have a sincere love for Jesus; I remember that I said to myself, "This is a very Godly man." He did not say so directly, but I eventually understood that he was trying to let me know that I might have driven more people away from Jesus that morning than I drew to Him. Of course, he did not use those words because he was much too gracious, but that was the gist of what I was hearing. So I said, "Mr. Barram, I just want people to know Jesus. Do you know a better way?" I will always remember his answer because it was life-changing. He said, "I don't know if I know a better way, but I do know another way."

That intrigued me because I thought he was speaking about another evangelism tool, like the Four Spiritual Laws. I used that booklet often; I also knew the Young Life approach and was greatly influenced by the Navigators' philosophy of ministry. In addition, I had taught a Sunday School class on "Lifestyle Evangelism" using a book by Dr. Joe Aldrich. Thinking he was speaking about an evangelism method of which I was unaware, I asked him to describe what he meant by "another way." He said it would take more than a paragraph or two, but he would be willing to spend some time with me if I was interested. He was so thoughtful and Christ-centered, I immediately knew that I would benefit from spending time with him. When I indicated my desire to do so, he said, "Why don't you meet me in my office, Tuesday morning at seven am?"

I showed up at his office promptly at seven. As I walked in, he greeted me and said, "I'm glad you came." Then, without explanation, he turned and walked over to a wall that had a floor-to-ceiling map of California on it. It appeared to have been pieced together from AAA maps. Dick looked at the top of the map and said, "Lord, you know Dave up there in Eureka is having serious problems with his boys. He really loves you and needs your help right now. Would you please help him with that family situation, especially with Tom?" Over the next hour, he proceeded to pray for people and officials in city after city, all the way to San Diego. When he finished, he said, "Okay, I'll see you next Tuesday."

My initial internal response was disappointment: "This is another way?" However, I was so impressed by his love of Jesus and people across the state that I came back the next Tuesday. My early disappointment stemmed from the fact that he didn't seem to have an action plan and I was a man of action. However, as the weeks and months passed, I learned that he was involved in a multitude of activities, but they originated from his prayer life. It wasn't that Dick did not talk to people about Jesus, because he certainly did; it was just that his approach was more Spirit-led and understated than mine. Week after week, we prayed for the state and people we knew, and I learned a new way of thinking. My walk with Jesus was becoming more personal and meaningful as we continued to meet every Tuesday morning.

A couple of years before I met him, Dick had been a pastor in Chico, California. He had responded to God's call to leave the pastorate and initiate a ministry to the legislators at the State Capitol and to business leaders in Sacramento. I was only one of the fortunate beneficiaries of his ministry. What I thought was a chance meeting turned out to be a God-ordained appointment. The conversations and activities we shared changed the direction of my life and ministry. I worked for myself in commercial real estate and could plan my schedule, so we often spent entire days together. Frequently, I drove Dick to Modesto, Stockton, or other cities around Sacramento. When we traveled, he often unexpectedly started praying for someone in the city we were passing. I remember one time we were going to Bakersfield and as we passed through Turlock, Dick started praying out loud: "Jesus, Mayor Kristofferson is embattled in City Hall because of his faith. Would you please encourage and strengthen him today?" That lasted about thirty seconds; then we continued our conversation as we drove down Highway 99. I learned to expect that and appreciate Dick's moment-by-moment heart connection with Jesus.

Increasingly, Dick invited me to accompany him in his ministry at the State Capitol. It was a real eye-opener to see how he communicated with legislators on a personal level. We would walk the halls praying on sight for people we met. As we felt the Holy Spirit's prompt, we would stop unannounced at a senator or assemblyman's office. It seemed like Dick knew the names of all the receptionists and it was rare that we heard "the senator is too busy for a visit." If they were in, we were usually invited into their office. A normal meeting would only be five or ten minutes, and often they would ask him to pray for something. Occasionally, it would be a thirty- to forty-five-minute meeting with a legislator or staff member who was wrestling with a personal or political challenge. Those short, unplanned meetings were relationship building; they led to private appointments and small group meetings for Bible study.

I also joined Dick for the well-attended Bible study/fellowship gathering for legislators of both political parties at seven o'clock on Wednesday mornings. The group was committed to confidentiality, so personal and sensitive political matters were shared openly. The men developed a high degree of trust in each other, one that transcended political differences. When the legislature was deadlocked over the budget or some other significant issue, we included the matter in our prayer time. In fact, often the resolution was initiated by a discussion after our gathering adjourned. That group was also the sponsor of the annual Governor's Prayer Breakfast.

I started as one of the men with whom Dick met; over time, he welcomed me as a partner in the ministry. I became chairman of the board of Western States Fellowship, which was his non-profit. My wife Mary Ann became his bookkeeper and continued that role for over fifty years.

Dick was closely associated with the network of people who sponsored the Annual Presidential Prayer Breakfast in Washington DC. From time to time, congressmen, senators, and other friends from the East Coast would pass through Sacramento for a few days. They reinforced what I was learning from Dick, and I was immensely blessed to know them. Many came through on a regular basis; the most frequent visitors were Doug Coe, Dr. Richard Halverson, and Chuck Colson. Dick Barram was the embodiment of the words of Paul in 1st Thes. 2:8 when he said, "we shared with you not only the gospel but our own lives as well." Dick not only did that but also gave me his wonderful network of friends.

Dick's commitment to a life of prayer and his philosophy of ministry affected me the most. I had been involved with ministries that had logos and lots of printed material about how to carry out those ministries. Our activities often involved large public events with well-known speakers. On the other hand, Dick worked one on one and with small groups. He typically stayed behind the scenes. He was off the radar, so to speak, but his life reflected the famous Alcoholic Anonymous quote, "Attraction, not promotion." People were attracted to him because of his love for Jesus and them. I would say that he instilled these things in me more by example than by speaking about them.

After fourteen years of working closely with the prayer breakfast movement, Dick Barram, Doug Coe, and Dick Halverson asked me to become a full-time associate with the Prayer Breakfast Fellowship. I believe that was in mid-1978. They wanted me to focus on California and the Middle East. My heart knew immediately that it was what I should do, but I procrastinated. During that time, every two or three months my wife lovingly asked me, "Are you still thinking about what Doug Coe and Dick Halverson asked you to do?" Of course I was, almost every day, but the fear of the unknown kept me from making that decision. However, in 1980, through a wonderful series of God-arranged circumstances, I made the commitment to become an associate with the ministry of Western States Fellowship. For a few more years, it was a tremendous privilege and honor to work alongside Dick. As his retirement drew closer, we had several serious discussions about the approaching transition. During our last meeting, we had a time of prayer; he gave me his blessing and handed the ministry over to me.

Dick Barram was one of a kind and is one of the unsung heroes in the family of Christ. Doug Coe often introduced Dick as "a man who actually does what we talk about." Often, the closer one gets to a person, the less heroic they become but that was not true of Dick. The closer one got to him, the more one admired him because his faith in Jesus was so authentic. One of the greatest gifts of my life was to know him as a mentor, brother, and friend.

His dedication to praying for people didn't end when he left California. After he retired, I visited him in Walla Walla, Washington. There, he had exchanged a map of California for a map of the world, and he prayed for one continent each day. When he went home to be with the Lord in 2003, I'm sure he heard, "Well done, my good and faithful servant."

I think you can see why I loved him and why this chapter has been about "a man who changed the direction of my life." I often think about those years we had together, and I miss him. When I think of Dick, I remember the statement in John 3:30 where the Apostle, speaking of Jesus, spoke these words: "He must increase but, I must decrease." Dick embodied that, and I am grateful for the years during which I had the privilege of working with and learning from him.

Conversation with an Agent-Promoter for Individuals and Groups

A friend introduced me to a man who was the agent for several well-known singers and rock bands. I will not mention the correct names but think along the lines of The Eagles, Bono, and Paul McCartney and you will understand the types of clients he had. We thoroughly enjoyed each other's company; it was one of those situations in which we liked each other immediately, so we began to meet weekly for lunch.

After several weeks, one of our lunches took us to a new level. As usual, our conversation was enjoyable and full of interesting subjects. Then, as often happens, we eventually focused on one topic. This day, it started with something we had both heard on the news. It was a survey asking people what they thought were the most significant problems facing our nation. The following is a very abbreviated version of the conversation that followed.

I asked, "How would you have answered that question? What do you think are the most serious problems that our country faces?

He said, "I would have a hard time choosing just one because there are so many that are damaging our country. Take your pick, crime, drugs, racial tension, political corruption, or a dozen other things, and now we have terrorism."

I replied, "You're right. We've had a war on drugs and passed civil rights legislation and the three-strike law for crime, but they continue to be major problems. I think of each of those as a symptom of an underlying cause that we are failing to address. When the body has an abnormally high temperature, we try to reduce it but realize that it is a symptom of something going on internally. It's just alerting us to find out what caused it."

He answered, "I guess you're right; all problems are caused by something."

I said; "Terrorism is caused by religious intolerance. I'm pretty sure each of society's other problems is also a symptom of a deeper issue. If that's true, I wonder if it's possible that there could be a common cause. What do you think?"

He said, "Maybe it's because the morality of the country is deteriorating; I know it's changed since I was a kid. I told you about my partner who ripped me off for more than a million dollars, and just two weeks ago, my daughter's bicycle was stolen from our front porch."

"What do you think caused such a general breakdown of our morals?"

"I don't know; maybe it's because there's so much corruption among our leaders in business and politics."

"Do you think corporations or politics are the problem, or is it the character of the individuals involved?"

"I see what you're getting at; of course it's the individual person who has a moral breakdown."

"If personal morality is the issue, who do you think is the greatest moral authority and teacher who ever lived?"

"I'm sure it was probably Jesus."

"Do you know much about what He taught?"

"No. I went to church when I was a kid, but never got too interested in religion."

"You know, that's my background too, but I was challenged some years ago to re-evaluate my ideas about spiritual things, and I'm so glad I did. I began reading the Bible for myself, and I started with the part that was written by the best friend of Jesus. In fact, why don't you and I read it together? We could read one chapter a week, then get together and discuss it. Would you be interested in that?"

"Yes, I think so, but I'm not interested in being pressured to believe a religious dogma."

"John, you can be sure I won't do that. I respect you and enjoy our friendship too much to allow any barrier to come between us. How about if we meet for breakfast every Thursday morning for five or six weeks? We already enjoy being together, so this should be fun. I'll get you a small copy of the book of John in modern-day English. We can each read the first chapter, and we'll talk about it."

"Okay, let's do it."

We met weekly for about a year and a half. His wife gave her life to Jesus, but my friend never did. He was too invested in New Age spirituality. In fact, the wall of his office contained pictures of seven Avatars, arranged in a semi-circle. Avatar comes from the Hindu religion and means a Savior who saves or rescues humanity. He had the pictures of Maharishi Mahesh Yogi and five others, plus Jesus. He did tell me that if he were ever to choose a personal Avatar, he would choose Jesus. That was encouraging, but in my judgment, he failed to understand or maybe refused to acknowledge the deity of Jesus.

After a couple of years, he moved to another area. Sadly, I don't see him anymore. I really liked him and would even say I loved him, so I still pray that he will someday come to a saving knowledge of Jesus.

A fascinating anecdote from our time together.

As our friendship developed, we shared numerous stories about our lives. One of the most interesting about his life was a meeting he and one of his clients had with Anwar Sadat, the president of Egypt. You may remember that in 1973, President Sadat led Egypt in an attack on Israel. It was called the Yom Kippur War, and Israel decisively defeated Egypt. Three years later, President Sadat humbled himself, visited Israel, and spoke to the Knesset. The Secretary-General of the Knesset, Netanel Lorch, an acquaintance of mine, arranged that visit. He told me that it was the high point of his life. Then they engaged in negotiations that led to the Egypt-Israel Peace Treaty being signed at Camp David. This won Sadat and Israeli Prime Minister Menachem

Begin the Nobel Peace Prize. Sadat was the first Muslim Nobel laureate.

In 1980, John and his high-profile client met with President Sadat and became captivated by his vision for peace in the Middle East. However, you may remember that in 1981 Islamic fundamentalist army officers assassinated President Sadat. The memory of that meeting stayed with them, so John and his friend talked about it often.

Twenty years later, they decided to honor Sadat's vision for peace by completing it. They had a number of ideas, one of which crystallized during the time I knew John, so I learned about it intimately. They were motivated by the idea of peace; the success of two of their friends led them to the method through which they thought it could be achieved. In 1985, Michael Jackson and Lionel Richie had written a song called "We are the World." Forty-five of America's top entertainers participated in the recording, which sold more than twenty million copies and received rave reviews around the world.

The memory of how that song brought people together became the model for their world peace plan. John and his client bought one hundred and sixty acres of beautiful land, hired an architect, and began planning the World Peace Center. Their intent was to produce a multitude of audio, video, and written projects by the entertainment and media industies. As we met week by week, I received updates on the progress of the architectural plans. Additionally, I heard the names of the most famous artists in the music industry who had volunteered to donate their time and talent to making videos and CDs promoting peace. This would be a very large project with significant buy-in from financial people as well as the most talented performers in the world.

Week by week, I was anxious to hear the latest developments. Then, one Thursday morning at breakfast, it all changed. John said, "We decided to sell the property." I was shocked and asked, "What happened to make you change your mind when so much progress has been accomplished?" He told me about a conversation he'd had the previous weekend. I knew that from time to time John's client picked him up with his Lear Jet and they spent the weekend together. John told me about his most recent flight to Vail, Colorado for a ski weekend. After several runs, he and his client were sitting in the warming hut at the top of the mountain discussing the project. All of a sudden, John had a very profound thought, which he shared with his friend. He said, "You don't have any peace, and I don't have any peace. How are we going to bring peace to the world?" And the dream died. That sounds like something a religious person might say to them, but John received that message internally. You and I know where that came from. They were working on peace between peoples of the world and were confronted with their lack of personal inner peace.

For several months afterward, I was allowed to read letters from his client. One of them was nine pages long. The letters were about the client's quest to find inner peace and the various places he had tried to find it. He talked about two books he had read and mentioned several retreats and conferences by New Age gurus. However, after each one, he concluded that they didn't have the answer. Then John's client died unexpectedly at fifty-three years of age. It was in a tragic accident, about a year or two after the dream died. I know that he was earnestly searching for inner peace, but I don't know if he was searching for God with his whole heart. However, if he was, I am confident the Lord would have revealed Himself to him before he died. Scripture confirms this:

"If you look for me wholeheartedly, you will find me." (Jeremiah 29:13 NLT")

"You will seek me and find me when you seek me with all your heart." (Jeremiah 29:13 ESV)

My purpose for sharing these conversations was simply to tell the story of two men who grappled with heart issues.

Conversation with an Angry Man

While hosting the five-man Palestinian delegation to the President's Prayer Breakfast, I experienced an unexpected turn of events that caused me to have a conversation with an extremely angry business executive. Let me give you the chain of events that led up to this man becoming a dear friend and brother in Jesus.

As I returned to the Hilton hotel, a good friend met me at the door and asked if I would meet with a man who was extremely upset because of something that happened during one of the events. Because I had been associated with the Prayer Breakfast for many years, my friend thought I should be the one to hear this man out. I was told that he was the president of one of America's largest corporations and that a meeting had already been arranged for four o'clock in the coffee shop. It wasn't what I had in mind for the afternoon, but I agreed.

When I was introduced to him, his hostility was palpable, and clearly indicated by his facial expression and body language. As we sat at a table, he said in a very aggressive, indignant tone of voice, "I didn't come here to be embarrassed by a TV preacher." Of course, that caught me off guard, so I asked, "What do you mean? What happened?" He acted like I should have known and asked, "Weren't you at lunch in the ballroom?" I answered, "No. I was over at the Capitol introducing some Middle East friends to several senators and congressmen. Would you please tell me what happened?"

He related the details of what had upset him. He said that a famous TV preacher was the speaker and had asked everyone to get on their knees and pray for the troops in Iraq. The moment I heard that, I felt an "oh no" in my spirit. While this mega-church pastor is a wonderful man, he was treating the gathering like a church service. It's true that the purpose of the Prayer Breakfast is to gather a cross-section of the world's leadership and lift up Jesus, but not in an overly religious or "churchy" manner. This pastor did not understand that the 2,500 people to whom he was speaking were as diverse as any audience in the world. They represented every political, economic, and religious view imaginable.

I asked, "Did you walk out?" He answered, "No, but I didn't get on my knees either." I said, "You are a better man than I am. I probably would have walked out." He was shocked and said, "Aren't you part of the leadership of this event?" I said, "Yes, I have been involved for almost forty years, but others are much more involved than I am." I explained that I was just trying to empathize with what he had felt at that lunch. I told him that I also had a strong aversion to being manipulated, and I gave an example. "I often go to church with friends who have a different worship style than I do. In their churches, the pastors say things like, 'If you love Jesus, raise your hands and give him a praise offering.' When that happens, I have a reaction similar to what you felt today. Even though the pastor may have good motives, I am put in a position of 'I do what they say or I don't love Jesus.' Well, I do love Jesus, but I have to admit that I refuse to be controlled by this approach."

This was a very simple metaphor, but it seemed to produce a softening of his attitude. We began a friendlier discussion. He asked me how I got involved with the Prayer Breakfast. I gave him the short version. I told him the history of the breakfast; he was fascinated by the details about how President Dwight Eisenhower and Senator Frank Carlson had initiated the first Presidential Prayer Breakfast in 1953.

After about an hour and a half of a very pleasant conversation, we agreed that we had better join our wives for the dinner. As we left the coffee shop, he asked if we could continue our conversation at a later date. He said that he would like to fly himself and his wife to Sacramento to have lunch or dinner with my wife and me. We agreed on a date and I didn't see him again until we met in Sacramento.

A week later, Mike and Heather arrived on their private jet and we took them to lunch. It could not have been a better or more enjoyable time. We each shared a bit about our families, places we had lived, etc. Mary Ann and Heather hit it off immediately and, of course, Mike wanted to continue the discussion we had started at the Hilton. That lunch lasted a little more than three hours. As we parted, Mike invited us to spend a week with him and Heather at their home in Palm Springs. Mary Ann could not make it, but I accepted and started to pray that this would be a life-changing week for Mike.

At that lunch, I learned that while we were in the Hilton coffee shop, Heather had been in her room praying and crying. She had been a follower of Jesus for a few years, but Mike had resisted all her attempts to interest him in anything spiritual. She was elated that he had accepted the invitation to attend the Presidential Prayer Breakfast even though she knew he was motivated by the presence of the President. He had also learned that most of the nation's legislators, plus leaders from one hundred and seventy nations, would be attending. However, now Mike was even more opposed to "the God thing," as he called it, and Heather was devastated.

Three weeks later, I flew to Los Angeles and we drove together to Palm Springs. About twenty minutes after we left their beautiful home, Mike started asking questions about God. He didn't have a negative attitude but rather seemed to be asking heartfelt questions.

When we arrived at the gated community where they had a second home, I recognized it because I had been there several times. In fact, I knew the golf pro at the club and one other family that lived there on a permanent basis. Mike and Heather were very well known at the clubhouse, where we ate many of our meals. They were genuinely surprised when a couple they knew quite well came over to greet me. In fact, I had stayed in that couple's home some years earlier and their situation was quite similar. The wife had become a believer but her secular Jewish husband had resisted her attempts to convert him. He had been willing to join a men's' group that I started in the desert and it was there that he had met Jesus.

Mike's questions continued. Some of them were difficult, like, "Where is God when villages in war zones are bombed, and women and children die?" My response was, "I don't know the answer to that, but I know that He loves those people as much as He loves you and I, so his heart must break over how evil is ravaging His world." Much later we had a very thorough discussion of the origin of evil and how God will judge it in the end. Though Mike was wrestling with difficult questions, they seemed genuine and the kind of questions that many thoughtful men had. After four days of this, the Holy Spirit opened the eyes of Mike's heart; I can't say it was any one thing but rather simply God responding to a hungry heart. In fact, Mike later said several times, "I knew I had a hole in my heart, but I just didn't know what to do about it."

Late on the evening of the fourth day, it happened. We were sitting by their pool, quietly chatting, when all resistance and questions vanished. Mike said, "I am ready to surrender my life to Jesus."

Heather and I held hands with Mike as he spoke earnestly to God, haltingly at first, using words that seemed difficult to form. I have come to realize that this is quite normal for a person who has never prayed. However, near the end of his prayer, tears started to flow as Mike became more comfortable speaking to God. I don't remember his words, but I do remember quite vividly his sincerity. Heather and I were also crying and there was a lot of hugging. It was a beautiful, sacred moment that I will never forget.

The years that followed were also beautiful to behold. Mike developed a heart for the poor of the world and became very generous with his funds. This led him to volunteer as a board member for a well-known international relief agency, which he still serves. As I reflect back on that day at the Hilton, I now view it differently. Though that pastor probably should have taken a different approach, God turned a negative into a positive as He began the process of drawing Mike to Himself.

Conversation with a Banker

The president of a large bank in San Francisco called me and said that a mutual friend of ours had encouraged him to meet me. The name he mentioned was a very close friend, so I was eager to know this gentleman. After a few minutes of small talk, we discovered that we had several other friends in common. One was on his board and was his weekly golfing buddy. Seeming to have an instant rapport, we began to check our calendars to see when we could meet. He and I were both motivated, so we were able to set a date within a week.

Our first meeting is all I'm going to describe, but it was rather unusual, so I wanted to add it to my growing list of *"Memorable Conversations."* To avoid breaching the confidential nature of our conversation, I will refrain from giving any hint of whom I'm talking about. After the initial get-acquainted necessities were out the way, I asked him why he and our mutual friend thought we should meet. It took a little time and patience, but the following is the bottom line of what I learned.

Some months earlier, he had contracted with a firm that specialized in team building. This firm spent three months meeting with people at the main office as well as all the branches. He had special one-on-one meetings with the president of that company, and after a month or two they had become quite friendly. Eventually, this man told him that to fulfill his potential as a leader, he had to discover his true self. That meant he had to operate out of his spiritual center. I will stop there, but you will understand where that led by knowing the following. It's reported that last year major corporations spent four billion dollars on team-building exercises, which range from the ropes course to classroom lectures. Many of these companies are based on New Age philosophy; this is what my new friend had brought into his bank. The turning point for him was when the head of the company tried to convince him that at the center of his being was divinity. He didn't have a spiritual background, but that sounded weird to him, so he rejected the premise and terminated the contract. Upon hearing this story, our mutual friend had strongly encouraged him to meet with me.

After understanding why he wanted to meet, I became very interested in knowing more about him. I asked him to tell me a bit about his background. Like most men, he was reticent to talk about himself, so I had to ask questions to learn the following. I will sum up about thirty minutes of our dialogue. He had a Harvard MBA, was president of a highly successful bank, made more money than he ever thought he would make, was married to a beautiful woman, had four children, lived in Marin County, belonged to the top clubs in the city, etc. Mind you, he did not volunteer all this easily; it took a series of questions. His recent experience, plus some things our mutual friend had told me, caused me to think that he was searching for something. He wasn't able to frame the question "Is that all there is?" However, that was what I was hearing.

I said, "Let me run an idea by you and see what you think about it. It sounds like you might be going through what many people call a 'mid-life crisis.' I don't care for that term and don't think it's helpful; I like the term 'mid-life evaluation' better. You can have a crisis if you make some dumb decisions while going through it, but it can also be a very positive time in life. I know that personally because I've been through it twice. You look back at your life experiences, evaluating what you're good at and what you don't want to repeat. Then you look forward and think, *How many good years do I have left? Do I need to make any changes to maximize and get the most out of those years?* A jet airplane that's off-course one degree for an hour is a long way off course, but not as much as it would be if it continued one degree off course for a day. Life can be like that, so a 'mid-life course correction' is in order from time to time. Does that sound like what you're thinking?"

He quickly said, "Yes," so I offered to spend some regular time with him and help him process his "mid-life evaluation." He said, "I would like that, how much do you charge?" I responded by saying, "I was offering to meet as a friend, and friends don't charge friends." He was incredulous and said that he would have to pay me. However, when I was unwavering in the offer of friendship, he relented, and we got out our calendars. After we settled on a date, he wanted me to meet his executive assistant for future appointments. After she left, we chatted for a few more minutes, then said goodbye. As I was opening his door to leave, I heard a very harsh voice say, "I don't want to talk about God or none of that ----."

Frankly, I was shocked at how strong his statement was, but I turned around, went back, and sat down. I said, "That would not be my purpose in being your friend, but now that you have brought it up, let me be candid about who I am. Let's say your new friend was Tiger Woods rather than me. Do you think you could become his good friend and he would never utter the word 'golf' in your presence? That would be impossible because golf is central to his life." I looked him straight in the eye and said, "Jesus is central to my life, so it would not be possible for us to be friends without your knowing that. However, you would probably also learn that I have ten grandkids and ten great-grandkids, that I love barbecue, and that I have a passion for golf. Our friendship wouldn't require you to love everything I love. In fact, I would learn a lot of those same things about you as well."

He answered, "Under those circumstances that would be all right."

That first meeting went so well, we continued to meet. Now every time we meet, he is the one who wants to talk about God. I think his encounter with a New Age guru caused him to do some soul-searching.

This was not the first time I had seen God use experiences like that. Another man with whom I meet had a short conversation with one of those religious groups where two of them knock on your door. That caused him to ask me questions about them. This, in turn, gave me the opportunity to fully explain the gospel to him. He is now following Jesus.

Conversation with a Golf Pro

For many years I regularly visited Palm Springs to spend time with the small groups we had initiated there. I often stayed in one of the exclusive gated golfing communities with a man and his wife. Bernie, whom I had met with for a number of years in the San Francisco Bay Area had been a non-religious Jew and could even have been characterized as an agnostic. As often happens, the Holy Spirit began to work in his life, and he eventually surrendered his life to Jesus. At age seventy-four, he decided to sell his business and retire to Palm Springs. He joined one of our small groups, and I visited him twice a year.

During one of those visits, he and his wife invited friends to their home for a catered dinner and to listen to their houseguest give a talk about God. Considering the fact that the invitation was word of mouth and that they didn't know who would be speaking, the couple's friends must have had a high regard for them, because eighty guests showed up.

The introduction Bernie gave me ended with him insisting that I tell them the story about my meeting with the Chief Rabbi of Israel. I did share that story briefly, then amplified its content as a lead into my talk about Jesus. It was well received and led to about twenty minutes of discussion. Doug, the head golf pro at the couple's club, stayed until nearly everyone left, then approached me and said he would like to have a private meeting if I had time. I invited him over the next afternoon.

When I asked what he wanted to talk about, he said that for some time he had been thinking that even though he believed in God, something was missing in his life. He said, "For the last six months I have been thinking about God nearly every day. Something happened to me last night when you were speaking about Jesus." After a couple of hours of my explaining the gospel and answering questions, he said, "I want to know Jesus like you're talking about, but I don't know how to do it."

I told him that many years ago I thought there was a specific "sinners prayer" that was necessary for salvation. "However, the Bible doesn't support that; God just wants to hear your prayer. To me, the examples of people whose sins Jesus forgave is indisputable proof of that fact.

"There are many examples, but I will mention just four: 1. One man who was a corrupt tax collector could not even look up toward God. With head down, he simply said, 'God, please have mercy on me, for I am a sinner.' Jesus said that the man went home 'right with God.' (Lk 18:13-14) 2. Two thieves were crucified on either side of Jesus. The one who recognized Him as the Son of God said, 'Lord, would you remember me when you come into your kingdom?' Jesus answered him and said, 'Today you will be with me in paradise.' (Lk 23:39-43) 3. It's important to also know about the man whose four friends carried him to Jesus. They made a hole in the roof (Likely removed tiles) and let him down right in front of Jesus while He was teaching. The man didn't say anything, but Jesus understood his heart and said, 'Young man, your sins are forgiven. Get up and walk.' (Lk 5:17-26) 4. A woman who was deeply moved by being in the presence of Jesus began to cry, and her tears dripped on his feet. She said nothing as she wiped them with her hair, but Jesus saw this and understood her heart. He said to the woman, 'Your sins are forgiven because your faith has saved you. Go in peace.' (Lk 7: 36-50)

"Do you get the point? The prayer that God accepts is the one that comes from the depths of your heart. You saw that in some cases no words were spoken; in others there was a heartfelt verbal recognition of the need to be accepted by God. However, they all had one thing in common; they had opened their hearts to Jesus; He knew that and gave them eternal life.

"What each of them felt but likely didn't understand at the time was that the Holy Spirit was giving them faith in Jesus. It appears this is what has been happening to you these past months. Now it is your turn to respond to the work of the Holy Spirit in your life. In light of the examples I gave, you know that Jesus understands your heart right now, so what do you think He is seeing?" He said, "I think he saw that I opened my heart to Him while we were talking." Then he said, "But I don't want to be a person who remains silent." I encouraged him to tell God what was in his mind right then. We bowed our heads, and here are the words he prayed with earnestness and sincerity.

"Our Father which art in heaven, Hallowed be thy name. Thy kingdom come. Thy will be done in earth, as it is in heaven. Give us this day our daily bread. And forgive us our debts, as we forgive our debtors. And lead us not into temptation, but deliver us from evil: For thine is the kingdom, and the power, and the glory, forever. Amen.

Then he looked up at me and said, "Can we go tell the Kaplans that I'm saved?" I said, "Sure, let's go tell them so they can rejoice with us." When he told them what had just happened to him, they did rejoice and said they had been praying for us the entire time we were in my suite.

This salvation story may sound a bit unusual, and it was a first for me, but the man had attended Catholic schools and that was the prayer that sprang out of his heart at that moment. You might think he didn't follow the formula of the so-called "Four Spiritual Laws" or the "Romans Road." However, I learned a long time ago that in the Scriptures, every person's interaction with Jesus is unique. In fact, not only did He forgive sins in a uniquely personal way, it was also the same when he healed someone. Think about this; every encounter with Jesus was one of a kind.

That was several years ago. By every indication, Doug genuinely met Jesus that day. I don't go to the desert anymore, but I pray that the small group he joined is helping him grow spiritually.

Postscript:

In the months that followed, Doug and I had several wonderful rounds of golf. Because he was a great teacher, he was able to give me a few pointers that helped improve my game. When I thanked him for his help, he insisted that this was not an equal exchange. I said, "I understand what you mean because of the smile on your face and the joy in your heart."

Conversations with a Mentor

I have been blessed to have had a number of very significant men invest in my life. Some of them have been world-class but not well known, while others were highly placed and internationally famous. I marvel at how God has directed my path and arranged for me to know and be influenced by these men. I could write about each of them (and probably will), but this article is about Dr. Richard (Dick) Halverson. Dick's words of encouragement, as well as his reproofs and thought-provoking questions, shaped my life. I was fortunate to have had him as a mentor because he was one of the most Christ-centered men I have ever known. In fact, though he has been gone for more than twenty years, he is still influencing me because I am currently re-reading his book, *The Timelessness of Jesus Christ.*

A short biography of Dick will help you understand a bit about the man who had such a tremendous influence on my life. When I first met Dick in 1964, he was a pastor in Bethesda, Maryland, which is a suburb of Washington DC. He left the pastorate after twenty-three years when he was appointed chaplain of the United States Senate. He held that position from 1981 until a few months before his death in 1995. He authored fifteen books and wrote the introduction for *My Utmost for His Highest* by Oswald Chambers. That was a good choice because Dick read Oswald every day for sixty years.

There is much that I could share here, but to keep this short, I will relate just a few of the encounters that dramatically redirected my spiritual journey. Not long after we met, Dick noticed that I was overly focused on evangelism and discipleship. A para-church ministry had taught me that this was the goal of a Christ-centered life. Dick helped me understand that the goal of a Christ-Centered life is a "Christ-centered life." I was not aware that I was focused on the secondary, but Dick sensed that men, rather than God, had called me to that focus. Only a person who loves you will speak truth into your life. Scripture confirms that: *"Faithful are the wounds of a friend."* (Pro. 27:6)

Let me relate a conversation we had that illustrates this point. Dick had the gift of discernment and exhortation, and he could be very direct. His preferred method of communication was a question, which he would answer himself.

On this day he said, "Glenn, your evangelistic agenda is so strong, it prompts me to ask: Was Jesus an evangelist?"

Then he said firmly, "No, He was not an evangelist.

"Was He a healer? No, He was not a healer.

"Was He a social worker? No, He was not a social worker."

Then he asked a question that I was supposed to answer. "Who was Jesus?"

"He was the son of God," I answered.

"That's correct. So, as the Son of God, what did he think about when He got up in the morning? Did He think, *I'm going to bring someone into the Kingdom*, or *I'm going to heal someone today* or *I'm going to feed people today*? No, these were not His focuses. His only thought was, *What is my Father's will?* His ministry flowed out that." Then Dick looked me straight in the eye and said, "Why don't you try to think, speak, and act like Jesus rather than the founder of an evangelistic ministry? That means you would need to get rid of your agenda and listen to the will of your heavenly Father, moment by moment."

That encounter led me to desire a Spirit-directed life, and God has graciously taught me how to walk in the Spirit. Evangelism/discipleship still happens, but it is not my focus. Jesus is.

Dick was normally very encouraging, but as I've said, he loved enough to confront as well. On another occasion, we were discussing some minor theological point...well, maybe it was a debate. I have already said he was the most Christ-centered man I've ever known, and I was debating him. Oh, the foolishness of a young man.

He looked at me as if he had just discovered something wonderful about me and said, "Glenn, I think you know more theology than the Apostles knew." I remember that for a millisecond I actually thought he was affirming my knowledge of Scripture. Then I realized, no, he had just stuck a knife in my gut and twisted it to let out a little spiritual pride. There wasn't much conversation after that. What could I say when I had just been devastated by a man I respected so greatly? Again, "Faithful are the wounds of a friend." (Pro. 27:6)

As I was driving away after dropping him off at his hotel, I had a series of thoughts out of nowhere that truly stunned me. "I do know more theology than the Apostles knew." They didn't have the inspired teaching of Paul about salvation by grace, spiritual gifts, the church epistles, or the Second Coming of Christ. They didn't have the unfolding of future events from the vision given to an elderly John on the Isle of Patmos. Then reality quickly set in. While they didn't have Romans, Corinthians, the Revelation, etc., they had something more vital and dynamic with Jesus than I had. My salvation wasn't in doubt, but I began to think about the fact that while I knew more information than they did, they knew Jesus in a way that I had not yet discovered. That produced a longing for intimacy with Jesus – an intimacy that I had only heard about. I began to constantly think and pray about how I could achieve that intimacy.

Some months later, I was the speaker at Woodleaf, a Young Life High School camp in Northern California. One morning, at daybreak, I went up on the hill behind the speaker's cabin to prepare for the day. As I sat against a tree, a verse jumped into my head. "Whatever was to my profit I now consider loss for the sake of Christ" and "I consider them rubbish that I may gain Christ." (Phil 3:7-8) At that moment, this verse became very personal and very real to me. Like Paul the Apostle, I decided that this was my heart's cry. Without any previous thought, I involuntarily held out my cupped hands. In a symbolic and metaphorical sense, they contained every doctrinal conviction I had, including the virgin birth, salvation by grace, etc. I lifted my hands to heaven, started to weep, and said out loud, "I will trade all of these for a heart connection with Jesus like the Apostles had." It seems clear to me now that the Lord took me at my word and began a process that continues until the present.* While not one of my doctrinal convictions changed, this had to happen so I could move beyond right doctrine and commitment to intimacy with Jesus.

It would take a book to explain all I learned from Dick. The intent of these abridged comments is simply to remember, honor, and publically thank my friend and mentor, Dick Halverson.

*For more details about how God led me after this experience, read my paper, "Re-Examining the Gospels" on my website, glennmurray.net.

Conversation with God about Myself

As I reflected on my most memorable conversations, one came to mind that I had not thought about for many years. It was a conversation that I had with God about my life. A little personal history will set the stage for why this internal conversation was so crucial for me.

After moving to Grass Valley, I started several weekly Bible reading/discussion groups with the leaders of our community. This effort eventually grew to fifteen men's groups, with ten individuals in each. The groups met in coffee shops, hotels, the hospital, pizza restaurants, two dental offices, and three country clubs. There were also two women's groups that I initiated but did not attend. For details about the history of these groups, read, "Conversation About the Grass Valley Groups." At the same time, I was involved with a weekly Bible study for legislators at the state capitol, bi-weekly groups in San Francisco, and twice-a-year trips to Seoul, South Korea. All of these were contributing factors to the following.

One Wednesday morning I attended the 6 a.m. doctors' group at the hospital, then moved to a coffee shop for my eight o'clock meeting with another group. Later that morning, I was driving to San Francisco to meet with a group in the Bankers Club at the top of the Bank of America building. As I passed the subdivision where I lived, I thought about the group that met at Alta Sierra Country Club. It was one of the most vital groups. As I continued to drive toward the Bay Area, I was praying for a friend in Korea. Suddenly, I remembered a phrase that I had heard many times. I asked myself, "Am I a mile wide and an inch deep?" The possibility that this could be true was a tremendously sobering thought that troubled me. As I mentally assessed how varied and full my schedule had become, an open-ended conversation with God about my activities began.

At first, my thoughts were self-justifying because of all the positive things that were happening in people's lives. Then I began to think about the possibility that it might be better to devote my time to fewer people with more depth. I was especially close to the doctors and the group that met in the conference room at the country club, so that idea seemed appealing. It also had a certain logic because it would mean a lot less traveling. I admitted to God that I was now very confused about the way forward. I began to earnestly ask Him for wisdom and clarification about how He wanted me to invest my life.

An internal/external dialog followed that lasted a full three months. It involved discussions with my wife and the men in my core group and an ongoing conversation with God. After several weeks, I remembered that Paul had warned the Galatians: "Are you so foolish? After beginning by means of the Spirit, are you now trying to finish by means

133

of the flesh?" (Gal. 3:3 NIV) Though I believed all my current activities were prompted by God when I started them, I was now questioning whether that was still true.

About halfway through this process I began to be impatient because I was not any closer to understanding what God wanted me to focus on. Then I started to realize that my thought process was flawed. I had been trying to decide which approach to ministry was best, but that was the wrong question. The idea that there was a "best way" arose because I had been heavily influenced by two para-church ministries. They insisted that giving one's life to a few is the Biblical model and backed it up with verses. I agree that there is great value in having a lifestyle of going deep with a few, but I began to ask a radical question: "Is that what God wants as the lifestyle of every believer?" I value my brothers who operate like that, but the resolution to my dilemma came when the Lord convinced me that the answer is a definite *no*.

Paul has a beautiful description of how all the parts of our physical body are different and how each is necessary. He emphasizes that the hand's role is different from that of the foot, etc. He uses that to illustrate how the Body of Christ operates. (1 Cor. 12:12-27 NIV) He is definitely speaking of spiritual gifts here, and to the best of my knowledge, I was operating in my spiritual gift. But God also created every individual with a unique personality. As I thought about that analogy, I became convinced that God had created me with the personality and motivation to be a catalyst rather than a maintainer. Then He called on me to paint on a broad canvas, and I was enjoying it immensely. While I did so, the possibility remained of going very deep with each individual. That has been my experience hundreds of times, often even during the first meeting.

I thank God for that drive to San Francisco during which He graciously initiated the process that caused me to be confident about the direction of my life. Paul's illustrations from 1 Cor. 12 helped me confirm who I am in Christ, and I am trying to be that daily. Since that time many years ago, God has provided me with the opportunity to speak to thousands of people in most of our nation's states and in more than seventy countries.

Now I can acknowledge to myself, "Yes, I'm a mile wide but not an inch deep." In fact, my life seems to be in sync with a famous quote: "If you want to irrigate broadly, dig a deep well." I have intimacy with Jesus and deep relationships with a few close friends. These friends and the Holy Spirit have confirmed my calling and released me to have a broad ministry.

Conversation with a Woman About Her Husband's Salvation

After I spoke at an event in San Francisco, a lady approached me with a request. We had never spoken but I knew who she was because she was very well-known in the city's financial circles. She mentioned the names of some mutual friends and said she had heard so much about me that she and her husband wanted to get to know me over dinner. I agreed to a time two weeks later, and her choice was one of San Francisco's finest restaurants.

When I arrived, she was already there and had arranged a private room. She apologized that her husband had been caught in traffic but said he would be there shortly. I sat down, and she immediately began to tell me about her husband. He was a wonderful man, but he had no interest in God, and she had been praying that he would "get saved." She went on to tell me that she had taken him to hear Benny Hinn and several other well-known evangelists but he was still "unsaved." Her super-spiritual language and some of the things she said caused me to think that several of the seed-faith evangelists on TV had heavily influenced her. It took just a few questions to confirm my suspicions. I thought to myself, 'Bet she sent them a lot of money.' I eventually understood that her concern for her husband's spiritual welfare was out of love and quite genuine. Then I started to wonder if her husband was rejecting the TV personality rather than God. Actually, that turned out to be very close to the truth.

After forty-five minutes, Steve arrived and in my judgment was making a statement that he did not want to be there. His wife jumped up and hugged him, saying, "Oh, Steve, I am so glad you finally got here. I've been talking with Glenn, and I think he is the man who can save you." Hoping she could not hear me, I turned to him and quietly said, "I am really going to disappoint your wife tonight because that is not who I am." He said, "Oh really? Who are you?" Of course, that made it even more awkward. The only thing I could think to say was, "I live in Grass Valley, and I come to the city often to visit my friends." He asked, "Who are your friends?" Since I have many, I thought for a moment about whom I should mention. I now know that the Lord prompted me to say just the right person. I said, "The first person who comes to mind is the president of a certain company," and I mentioned him by name. Steve's face softened. He smiled and said, "I'm his personal attorney and on the board of his company." That seemed to break the ice; we talked about their common love for golf and a number of other things. When I told Steve that we had played golf several times, he invited me to play golf with him at the San Francisco Golf Club. I took him up on it, and we became friends.

Our friendship seemed very genuine though it started in such a bizarre manner. He was an attorney but spent most of his time on an investment group he had put together. They invested exclusively in Asia, and because I traveled to China from time to time, I invited him to go with me to play golf with the Vice Premier. He was very excited about that, but unfortunately was unable to go due to a couple of broken ribs. However, we continued to meet regularly, and before long, he was asking questions about God. One day we were in a very substantial discussion, and it seemed to be helping him. In the middle of our conversation, he got an urgent phone call that made him leave immediately. He was frustrated and said, "Next time we meet, could we spend the whole day talking about God?" Of course, we did that, then had dinner as well. That was a marathon day of talking about Jesus.

Then about eighteen months after we met, there was that special day we were having lunch at his private men's club. A former Secretary of State was having lunch at the table next to ours. Steve knew the man, so they chatted for a few minutes before he sat down with me. As we were looking at the menu, I started to feel God prompting me that this was the day to be very direct with Steve.

After the soup had been served, I said, "Steve, you and I have had some very deep discussions, and I have come to believe that your questions have mostly been resolved. I think today is the day you should surrender your life to Jesus, and I think it is right at this table that you should do it. You know all the right words already, and we have talked about the fact that you don't need to close your eyes to pray. So why don't you make this the day that you become a child of God? It might even be fun to mark the day in your memory as the day you received Jesus while sitting at a table next to your friend, the former Secretary of State, and he didn't know you were praying. You can pray silently with your eyes open because all you need to do is open your heart to Jesus. It's your call, but I am going to eat my soup now."

He was silent while I ate my soup. Then he said, with real conviction, "I did it." In the following months, it seemed obvious that God had heard Steve's silent prayer and made him a new creation in Christ.

Later, while attending an elegant party at the same private club, his wife said she was unsure that Steve had been saved because he didn't sound like it. I felt strongly that I should be very forthright and candid with her. I said, "Steve will likely never be a 'praise the Lord' type of guy or say 'hallelujah' or 'glory' like you do, but then neither do I and I know for certain that I'm 'In Christ.'" I would like to report that this put her mind at rest about Steve going to heaven, but I doubt it.

However, I consider Steve a brother in Christ, and we continue to meet.

Conversation with an Exhausted Ministry Leader

Some time ago, I received a phone call from a good friend who wanted to talk. We laughed and remembered past experiences, but eventually the conversation turned to how he was doing. For many years, Jack had led the U.S. division of one of the largest international ministries. After over an hour of him sharing serious challenges that the ministry faced and then numerous details about his own life, I suggested that we pray for some of the issues before we continued. After I prayed, he started to pray but immediately broke down and began to sob. After several seconds, he said, "I guess you can tell I am not in a good place. I think I would really benefit from spending a couple of weeks with you. Would you be open to that?" I felt an immediate prompt from the Lord to say yes but told him I would need to check with my wife. Actually, I had some doubt as to whether I was the right person to help him. However, after Mary Ann and I prayed about it, we had peace about inviting him for a visit. We found the best time for us, contacted him, and set a date.

About three weeks later, he arrived at my home. We had a delightful lunch and a time of fellowship. Then we went to my office and began to unpack the load he was carrying. Actually, we spent the first two days just talking about his schedule and the pressure he faced. Most of the time I just listened, but during each session, I became more convinced that my friend was either depressed or, more likely, completely burned out and maybe even close to a collapse. I think it was the third morning that I sensed God would have me take a very different and highly unusual approach as I shared some thoughts with him. I warned him that I was going to do something that I had never done before and that it would be weird for both of us. Then I said:

"Jack, I'm Jesus, and I want you to know how upset I am with you. In many of the choices you've made, you have been following men instead of me. Let me explain what I mean. I called you to lead this ministry, and it is a full-time job, but you have allowed yourself to be influenced by what I am doing in other men's lives. You went to a conference, where a very Godly old man was speaking. He said that for most of his life he had risen at five o'clock every morning, studied the Scriptures, and taken notes so God would know he was paying attention. So you started doing that every day. Then you went to another retreat and a person you respected was encouraging everyone to follow Paul's admonition to Timothy: 'Teach what you have learned to trustworthy people who will be able to pass them on to others.' (2 Tim. 2:2) So you chose several men and have given them an enormous amount of your time. You agreed

141

to write a book about the history of your organization. After hearing Tony Campolo speak about the needs of the poor in Haiti, you committed to helping him raise financial support. With your wisdom and leadership ability, they asked you to serve on the Elder board of your church, and you accepted. Because you are a knowledgeable and articulate Bible teacher, your calendar is filled with speaking engagements. I will stop now, but I could add many other things that I did not ask you to do. I hope you get my point.

"I think all those things are wonderful; however, many of them are things I did not ask you to do. You have created such a structured life that the pressure is killing you. You've admitted that the load you're carrying is heavy, but I want to remind you that my burden is light. Some people would say that you are a classic case of over-commitment, but I want you to understand that it is more serious than that. You're so busy working for me that you can't respond to my daily guidance.

"I want you to stop everything you can, immediately, then responsibly fulfill your other commitments. However, as soon as possible, I want your calendar to be empty except for your responsibilities in leading this ministry. Stay in that condition for a week, a month, or maybe nine years and wait for me to speak to you. When the time is right, I will tell you what I want you to do, so just respond to my leading. From now on, you can appreciate and encourage the various things others are doing but don't assume I want you involved."

The next few days, we spent a lot of time discussing how to follow Jesus by responding to the check and prompt of the Holy Spirit. Jack wound up staying only ten days but left with a commitment to follow through on all we had talked about. He said he already felt a sense of freedom just anticipating what God had in store for him in the future.

Postscript:

Late-breaking update on Jack: He is still leading that great organization and says that while his workload is immense, he feels very little pressure. He believes the Lord has led him to continue some of his former activities but most of them are no longer on his calendar. His latest email ended with: "And my marriage has never been better."

Conversation with God
About San Francisco

We will get to my conversation with God later, but first a short history of my involvement in San Francisco. Walter Hoadley was president of the Federal Reserve Bank of Philadelphia when he was recruited to join Bank of America as executive vice president and chief economist. At that time, the bank's headquarters was in San Francisco. After he moved to the city, he initiated a small fellowship group that met in the bank's boardroom. It was a closed group that included Dick Burress (director of the Hoover Institution at Stanford), Judge Henry Rolph, Lee Soule (president of a steel company), Frank Haas (a developer of retirement communities in Florida), etc. Shortly after the group started, I was invited to join. One day a month, I drove from Grass Valley to the city for that breakfast. The rest of the day was spent in one-on-one meetings with these men. They all became very close friends, and years later I was honored to be a pallbearer at Walters's funeral. We eventually opened that group; depending on the morning, it continues to average between thirty to seventy businessmen. It also spun off dozens of small groups that meet weekly in someone's office.

After I had attended for about a year, Frank Haas and Walter challenged me to invest more of my time with the business leaders of San Francisco. They asked me to move to the city and said several of the men would cover the cost of our housing, an office, a car, an assistant, and a generous salary. After much prayer and discussion with my wife and the guys in my small group, I had no peace about moving to San Francisco. However, God had given me a love for the city and put an idea in my head about how to proceed. I told Frank and Walter that I would come to the city for three days every other week and maybe I would find the person who could be on site twenty-four-seven. That decision led to thirty-six years of ministry in the city, and after several false starts, just the right man was found. My time in the city also changed the direction of my life.

During my first visit to the city after this decision, I tried to discern what God would have me do for those three days every other week. Because I had a relationship with only a few men, I walked the streets praying. One thought kept returning: that I should pray for the city on Twin Peaks, which has a 360-degree view of the city. I responded to that; for several weeks, I drove into the city and immediately went up to Twin Peaks to look at the city and talk to God about it. The wonderful thing about that lookout area was that I could see the entire city very clearly laid out below me. It was prayer, of course, but it seemed more like I was simply chatting with the Lord because I was talking out loud with my eyes open. I would pray for specific buildings by mentioning them as "the gray one to the left of the Transamerica Building" or "that very tall one close to the bridge." I later came to believe that many of the relationships and events that took place over the next thirty plus years, were birthed on that mountain.

This was such a special experience that it motivated me to repeat it as I traveled the world. In more than seventy-five nations, I always found a mountain or the highest building and prayed for that city. In Seoul, it was Bugak Mountain, where God gave me a heart for Korea, which led me to visit Seoul fifty-five times. During those visits, God gave me favor and a very substantial ministry with dozens of business and political leaders, including six presidents.

As I prayed for San Francisco, I began to love the city of St. Francis, but still didn't have any direction about how God wanted me to interact with its leadership. As I continued to pray for the city, numerous ideas came and went, but one stood out above all the others. It was that I should walk around every large office building and ask God for a relationship with a person of responsibility in each. I knew that the idea was only a first step, but I was very excited about taking that step and trusting God for what to do after that.

I bought a small notebook and walked the streets, writing down the addresses and names of every large building, as well as a few smaller buildings like the Pacific Coast Stock Exchange, which seemed important. Then, for several months, I spent an hour or so in front of and walking around each of those buildings, talking to the Lord about the people inside. Sometimes I would recognize people because I had seen them entering or leaving several times. I assumed they were from that building, so I prayed for them specifically and wondered whether I would ever meet them. I kept track for several years and am thrilled to report that God gave me one or more friends in every one of those buildings. Each of those relationships has a story to tell, but I will share just one.

I remember well my first encounter with someone in one of those buildings. It happened because Walter introduced me to the president of a major corporation. The first meeting started awkwardly, but within a few minutes the man became incredibly vulnerable and shared many things about his personal life. We started to meet every time I was in town and became very good friends. Within three months, he surrendered his life to Jesus, and we started a fellowship group in his office with him and four of his peers.

After that, it seemed like every corporate executive I met wanted to introduce me to one or more of his friends. Within months, my calendar was full of men who, for the most part, were not believers but who, because a trusted friend had introduced me to them, often at lunch, were very open to meet. Leadership is a lonely and stressful position, and a very small number of leaders have anyone with whom to process the experience. Often, during the first appointment, I asked, "Can I quote you an ancient proverb and see if you identify with it? It goes like this:

"Oh the comfort, the inexpressible comfort of feeling safe with a person, having neither to weigh thoughts or measure words, just pour them all out, grain and chaff together, sure that a faithful hand will sift them, keep what is worth keeping and with the breath of kindness blow the rest away."

I then asked, "Do you have anyone in your life like that?" It didn't matter whether I asked a legislator, CEO, or pastor; I always heard something like, "Are you kidding me?" or "I would give anything for a friend like that." I offered them that kind of confidential friendship and stated categorically that I did not have a hidden agenda. Sometimes I added, "But if I were you, I wouldn't believe me until a large amount of trust has developed." Over many years, only one man didn't accept that offer.

Years before I came to San Francisco, my mentor Dick Halverson had a huge influence on me. He encouraged me to stop following the evangelistic formula of the Para-church ministry to which I was connected at the time. Instead, he challenged me to think, act, and speak more like Jesus, who had only one thought: "Responding to the will of the Father with every person He met." When I researched how He related to people, I found it clear that no encounter was like the previous one. In fact, every individual's experience was a unique, personalized encounter with Jesus. That meant, for every appointment, I had to learn to live by the prompt and check of the Spirit. Without condemnation of others who pursue the traditional ways of thinking about ministry, that has been my goal for the last forty years. The ministry to which I was called is the "Ministry of Presence," meaning

148

that for every appointment, my intent is to arrive full of the Holy Spirit and serve the agenda that develops between us. As I look back over the years, I recall that a multitude of people met Jesus personally, and countless others were encouraged to become serious disciples.

I could relate hundreds of stories about the wonderful things that resulted from those prayers on Twin Peaks, but my intent was simply to give praise and glory to God for allowing me to be His junior partner in a small part of what He wanted to accomplish in San Francisco.

Conversation with a Golf Shop Owner

Some time ago, I was the only customer in a golf store right after it opened. Several times, I glanced at the man behind the cash register; he looked depressed. Eventually, I felt certain that something was bothering him, so I said, "You're having a rough day, aren't you?"

He was a little shocked and said, "How did you know?"

"I don't, but I was watching you for a few minutes and I just felt like I should encourage you. Do you have a difficult situation going on?"

"Yes," he answered. "I just took my brother to the emergency room; he's vomiting blood. He's going to die if he doesn't get off the booze."

I still can't remember exactly what I said, but it must have been something like, "He needs to know Jesus."

He immediately asked, "Can we talk?"

Of course, I said "Yes." He was the store's owner, so he locked the front door and said, "Let's go upstairs to my office."

We talked for over two hours, and I will give you a synopsis. I asked him why he had responded so quickly when I said his brother needed to know Jesus. He said that he had been thinking a lot about Jesus himself recently. Because he was so open, I took the opportunity to explain the gospel to him in some detail. This included a lot of dialogue because while he had some basic knowledge, he also had a number of questions with which he was wrestling.

After an hour or so, he said, "I want to know Jesus like you do."

"Great! Some people would have you pray the so-called 'sinner's prayer,' but I think Jesus prefers you to pray your own prayer. You and I have discussed the basics of salvation, so why don't you tell God what's in your heart right now? Just talk to Him." I bowed my head and waited for what seemed like a minute or two; I didn't hear him say anything.

I thought he might have prayed silently, but when I looked up, he was looking at me. He asked, "Do I have to speak in tongues when I do this?"

I was surprised. "Why do you ask? We didn't discuss that."

He said, "I was at this same point with a man in Oregon ten years ago, and he said the minute I received Jesus I would start speaking in tongues, and that would be the evidence that Jesus was in my heart. It scared me, so I didn't pray."

I said, "I have never spoken in tongues, but am certain of my salvation. The Bible says that the Holy Spirit bears witness with our spirit that we are children of God. (Rom 8:16) That has happened to me, and it's all the evidence I need."

This was yet another example of a zealous person getting ahead of the Holy Spirit. I admit that in years past I had done this myself. When I was active in a Para-church ministry, I relied more on getting people to respond to the Four Spiritual Laws booklet than on being in sync with the Holy Spirit. I now believe that many of those I encouraged to pray the so-called "sinner's prayer" were spiritually "stillborn," not genuinely born again by the Spirit. I guess I knew at the time that people can be genuinely born again only when the Spirit draws them, but I was too focused on reporting how many people had prayed to receive Christ.

After much more conversation, this man gave his life to Jesus. Are you ready for the irony of this particular story? He sold his shop, and I lost track of him for about ten years. When he returned to visit his family, we met and had great fellowship. During the conversation, I learned that he was the pastor of a Calvary Chapel startup church in Southern California and that he spoke in tongues.

Conversations About Grass Valley Groups

In 1975, after living in Sacramento for many years, I felt led to move to Grass Valley, which is in the foothills of the Sierra Nevada Mountains. It's just sixty miles from our former house but feels like a thousand miles; we built a home in the suburbs on five beautiful, secluded acres of pines and oaks...and, yes, we have a trout stream in our front yard. Thank you, Jesus.

After we were settled and had found a good church, I began to think and pray about the ministry opportunities in our new community. One option was to continue the same ministries we had in Sacramento, but I felt a check, so we waited. One day I was a bit frustrated about not hearing from the Lord, so I went up on the mountain to a place that offered an overview of the entire area. I spent an hour or two just thinking and praying, and got very excited when an idea came to me. It was just the germ of an idea, but as I thought about the possibilities of its coming to fruition, I became excited. The idea was in the form of a question: How would I respond if an angel appeared to me and said, "Jesus is coming to Grass Valley for one day, and He wants you to arrange his schedule"?

A few days later, I was at that same spot with a yellow legal tablet. I was ready to do some thinking. Of course, I wouldn't want to waste His time, so I tried to think of every option. Soon, ideas flooded me. I thought, 'Maybe I should take him to the hospital and heal everyone. On the other hand, I could take him to the high school and change the lives of the future leaders of our community.' That appealed to me because for ten years I had led "Young Life Clubs" at three high schools in Sacramento and had learned to love high school kids. 'On the other hand, should I take him to every church? Maybe that would bring revival to our town.' These are just a few of the ideas I had, though one thought started to dominate my thinking.

The idea was to schedule thirty-minute appointments for Jesus with the most prominent leaders of our community. Of course, if I told them that Jesus was going to visit Grass Valley for one day, they would not believe me. However, I knew that if this were literally true, very few people would say no if I asked, "Would you like to have a thirty-minute meeting with Jesus?" I knew that everyone would want to meet Jesus, even if only out of curiosity. He would not be physically present, but because He is present in Spirit, I asked God for a plan that would accomplish this task. However, I had a small problem. I was new to the community and did not know who the candidates should be. I read the newspaper daily to evaluate who was well-known and influential.

Over the next several weeks I came up with a list: the senior judge, the chairman of the county Board of Supervisors, the editor of the newspaper, the manager of a well-known bank, the district attorney, the owner and manager of the radio station, the mayor, and several of the most prominent businessmen. I then prayed about how I would approach them and whom I should contact first. Again, my intent was to arrange for Jesus to have a thirty-minute meeting with each of these men.

A method of allowing this to happen began to form in my mind, so I went to the most unlikely person first. I called and told this person that I had an idea I wanted to present to him. I thought he would want to know what the idea was before I would be able to schedule the appointment but he agreed to Tuesday morning at 10 am.

The idea I shared with him was as follows: "I am new to the area, and I have been thinking about the leadership in our community. I have some experience working with those in leadership and I know the benefits and frustrations that accompany it." I told him: "After a little research, I learned that you are one of the most respected leaders in town, and I know that this is a very lonely place. I would like to propose that we start a breakfast group with you and nine other men who hold similar positions." I then mentioned the names of the men I was going to contact.

I explained that this breakfast group would be both a place to discuss the community's needs and a safe place to process personal issues. This would happen over time as our commitment to confidentiality allowed trust to develop among us. Then I quoted one of my favorite proverbs: "Oh the comfort, the inexpressible comfort of feeling safe with a person, having neither to weigh thoughts nor measure words, just pour them all out, grain and chaff together, sure that a faithful hand will sift them, keep what is worth keeping, and with the breath of kindness blow the rest away." Then I asked, "Do you have a place like that?"

He said, "It sounds like the relationships we had in my college fraternity years." I agreed and said, "It was your common commitment to each other and the fraternity that made it work. I was thinking about the common interest that would hold this group together. It is unlikely that they all belong to Rotary, or all play golf, or the other things that create a common bond. I was thinking that the best chance for this group to gel is if we meet in the spirit of Jesus." He immediately said, "I am not religious, and this idea doesn't appeal to me at all." I responded, "Great, because this will not be about religion." Then I asked, "Would you try it for four weeks? If it doesn't fit your schedule or is not enjoyable, you are free to stop, no questions asked." There was several seconds of uncomfortable silence. Then he swore and said, "####, I guess I could try it for four weeks." Later, after we had become good friends, he told me that he had decided to say yes because I had mentioned that I was going to contact our senior judge and the chairman of the County Board of Supervisors; he thought they might say yes and he would not be in the group. It seemed clear that God had gone before me and prepared each person because, without exception, every person on my list became part of our first breakfast group. That group still meets weekly and has done so for over thirty-eight years.

For our meeting place, I arranged a private room in a hotel for these nine men plus myself. For this group and every group that followed, I started with a restatement of what I had told each person, including that we would be meeting in the spirit of Jesus. Then, to remove the fear of the unknown, I explained a proposed format of a strict one-hour meeting, with the first thirty minutes focusing on current events and personal situations. I then told them I wanted them to think of the second thirty minutes as follows.

"Let's imagine that Jesus were speaking in person up at Scotts Flat Lake, which is about four miles outside of town. We could all go listen to what He had to say. Then, the next morning, we could have our breakfast and give our personal opinions about what we had heard. There would be no restrictions on what you could say because our breakfast would be a safe place to process how you felt about any issue. Because Jesus is not actually speaking at the lake, we would read a portion of what He had told other people at the Sea of Galilee. Jesus had a best friend who wrote a book about his life, so we will use that book to evaluate what He said to the people."

One of the more memorable moments from that first group was when we read the book of John and came to the passage where Jesus said to Nicodemus: "you must be born again." When we opened it for discussion, the first man to speak said, "Ever since Jimmy Carter was President, I've wondered what 'born again' means." Another man spoke up: "I would like to know also because my brother wrote me a letter three weeks ago and said I needed be born again." Because I had started the group, all eyes turned to me. One man said, "Glenn, what does it mean?" I approached each of the groups with the attitude that the Holy Spirit would be our teacher as we read the Scriptures. Therefore, my answer was: "Guys, I have an opinion about that but what if I am wrong? What is important is what Jesus means by that phrase. Let's read it again and see if we can decide what He means." After we reread it, there was complete silence, which was unusual in that group. I think everyone was afraid to give an opinion that might have been wrong. Eventually, I said, "Well, guys, I told you I have an opinion about that, but if you don't share what you think about that phrase, I am prepared to leave without sharing my view. Come on, now; you must have some thoughts after reading it twice."

Eventually, one man said, "Well, I guess it is like being born physically except it's different in some way." That seemed to be our only starting place, so I prompted them to explain the process of how one is born physically. They spent about ten minutes discussing that a boy and a girl get together and have intercourse, and she gets pregnant. That led to a discussion about abortion, miscarriage, the baby being stillborn, etc. Eventually, we got to a normal birth.

There was total silence, and then one man said, "I think I am about six months pregnant." I asked him what he meant by that statement, and his answer was a first for me. He said, "I've been in the group for about six months, and I don't know about being born again, but I feel like I'm about to give birth to something." Another guy spoke up: "I think I'm further along than you are." Within weeks, both of those men were genuinely born again. The first man who spoke up went on a men's retreat with me in Colorado, and it was there that he received the life of Jesus. Sadly, he died of cancer about eighteen months later, but happily, he is with Jesus.

Eventually, there were fifteen men's groups and three women's groups meeting with the same format. There was a group at all three country clubs, a doctors' group that met at 6 am at the hospital, a dentists' group, a nurses' group at the hospital, a group of men in law enforcement (including the city attorney, three judges, the sheriff, the captain of the California Highway Patrol, etc.), and a women's group in my home with my wife facilitating.

Following are some of the responses I received when I met individually with men for the first time. Remember that I had never met any of the men, so I had no knowledge of their spiritual interest. However, I gave each person essentially the same information about what the group would be like and said that we would be meeting in the spirit of Jesus. Two men said, "I've never read the Bible; would I feel uncomfortable there?" Another said, "I will join if you won't broadcast that I am attending." Another man said, "I am Jewish, but I would be interested in meeting with that group of men." For his group, we started with the book of Hebrews. Later he said, "I have learned more about the Jewish faith than I did for my bar mitzvah."

When I presented the idea to the chairman of the Board of Supervisors, he got tears in his eyes and said, "You don't know how much I need something like this. Sometimes after a late-night meeting that is especially difficult, I stop by the Episcopal church, which is the only one that leaves its doors open. I just go in and sit in the dark and try to recover my sanity." I later learned that he attended the Methodist church regularly and, of course, became a consistent attender until his death twenty-seven years later. It is still amazing to me that no one ever missed a breakfast unless they were ill or out of town. That group of most retired men, still meets weekly.

A group at one of the country clubs was possibly the most remarkable. Billy Graham says that after age seventy, one in a million people surrenders their life to Christ. That group was so amazing because every man was over seventy and six of them received Christ.

My appointment with the mayor went well until I said, "We will be meeting in the spirit of Jesus." He interrupted me and blurted out, "What the h… does that mean?" I was a little taken aback but gave him an honest reply. I said, "I'm not exactly sure because no one has ever asked me. However, I must mean something by it because I use it quite often. Let me think for a moment." I believe the

Lord then gave me an answer for him. I asked, "Have you ever heard of the Bible verse John 3:16?" He said, "Yes, I have seen it at football games and it's on that ham radio tower on Highway 49." I asked, "Do you know what it says?" He admitted that he did not, so I quoted it to him, and then asked, "Have you heard of John 3:17?" When he said, "No, I have never seen those numbers," I told him that this verse was just as important as 3:16 and I quoted it for him. *"...God did not send his Son into the world to condemn the world, but in order that the world might be saved through him."* I continued: "So, if we meet in the spirit of Jesus, you would not feel condemned, and if you did, it would not be from Him." Then, suddenly, he began to weep uncontrollably. At first, I thought I must have touched some deep-seated issue. I apologized but he quickly got it together and said, "Don't worry about it; that statement affected me to the core of my being because I have worried all my life about being condemned by Jesus." Of course, he joined one of the prayer breakfasts, and about two years later he surrendered his life to Jesus. Some years later, when he decided to move to San Diego, I was the first one who knew it because he called and asked if there was a group like ours down there. I assured him that there was and introduced him to my associate and longtime friend, Milt Richards.

When I met with another man who seemed very open, his countenance indicated that he was anxious to join the group. However, when I asked him to try it for four weeks, he very graciously said he would not be able to accept. He had given me the opposite reaction, so I told him that and wondered why he was saying no. His answer was, "You called this a prayer breakfast, and even though I am Catholic, I don't know how to pray in public." I asked him if he knew how to pray silently. He said yes, so I told him that was the same thing to God. He joined a group and became very Christ-centered; eventually, he became the facilitator of that group.

One of the prominent businessmen on my list owned three stores, one of which was the largest liquor store in the area. When I contacted him, he asked me to meet him at the liquor store. We went into the back room, where I sat on a case of Jack Daniels whiskey and invited him to join one of our breakfasts. Of course he accepted. The evening of his first meeting, he called me at home and said, "I'm in." I reminded him that he had four weeks to decide. He said, "I'm aware of that." When I asked why he was so sure, he said, "For years I've wondered if there was a place where I could ask questions about God without being condemned. I think this is the place." Within a year, both he and his wife were baptized at First Baptist Church and sold the liquor store.

As I stated earlier, we intentionally avoided an evangelistic approach so that each man would not feel like a target or as though they were being manipulated in any way. We just wanted them to have thirty minutes a week with Jesus because that was the vision He gave me. However, nearly every group started with approximately ninety percent nonbelievers; as I look back over the years, I believe that at least seventy percent met Jesus personally. When a number of the wives showed interest, we started a couples' Bible study in our home.

Within a few years, several of the people formed a committee and initiated an Annual Community Leaders Prayer Breakfast. It's held at a country club and has been a sell-out for the past thirty-plus years. Each year has a different theme, and the head table consists of people involved in that discipline, including the speaker. Here are some examples. We honored law enforcement, and the sherrif spoke about his spiritual journey. Another year we honored and prayed for those in politics, with our Congressman speaking about his faith in Jesus. Other years we honored medicine, firefighters and paramedics, education, social agencies, non-profits, etc.

These activities were the springboard the Lord used to prepare and send me around the globe to interact with the leaders of many nations.

Made in the USA
San Bernardino, CA
23 January 2020